THE GOD OF THE BIBLE

The God of the Bible

R T KENDALL

KINGSWAY PUBLICATIONS
EASTBOURNE

Front cover photo: Heinz Stucke, Frank Spooner Pictures

British Library Cataloguing in Publication Data

Kendall, R. T. (Robert Tillman), *1935–*
The God of the Bible.
1. Christian doctrine. God
I. Title
231

ISBN 0–86065–808–2

Printed in Great Britain for
KINGSWAY PUBLICATIONS LTD
1 St Anne's Road, Eastbourne, East Sussex BN21 3UN by
Courier International Ltd, Tiptree, Essex
Typeset by J&L Composition Ltd, Filey, North Yorkshire

To Lyndon

Contents

Preface

One of my greatest thrills in Britain has been giving Bible Readings at Spring Harvest. Spring Harvest is an Easter phenomenon which now attracts upwards of 60,000 people annually over three sites in Britain. It consists largely of seminars (prepared by Clive Calver and Stephen Gaukroger), lively worship (led by men like Dave Pope and Graham Kendrick), prayer, fellowship and fun. But its leaders see to it that the Bible readings form a vital part of the whole event. I am but one of a number of preachers who have been invited to share in this ministry.

This book is a report of my Spring Harvest Bible Readings from 1986 to 1989. They have been edited — but not a lot (which will be apparent!). They have followed the themes set by the organisers each year, hence the four divisions of this book. 'Deckchairs on the Titanic', the 1989 theme, is vintage Pete Meadows, one of the architectural minds of Spring Harvest. The Bible Readings follow the particular biblical book and chapters laid down by the Executive, but beyond that the preacher is given total liberty in dealing with a given passage. Therefore the reader should not hold the organisers responsible for the content!

The idea for this book was born at dinner in Skegness when Elizabeth Catherwood, a seminar speaker in 1988, and her son Christopher expressed their feelings that the influence of Spring Harvest should be extended beyond the bare event. I hope this book will give the reader a taste of at least one aspect of Spring Harvest and even provide a nostalgic 'replay' for those who may have actually sat under these biblical expositions during those memorable mornings.

A sweet fringe benefit of Spring Harvest has been to meet and enjoy a host of beautiful Christians I might not otherwise have known. Besides having the friendship of Clive Calver and Pete Meadows I have been enriched by men like Colin Saunders, David Evans, Dave Pope, Doug Barnett, Mike Morris and many others. But I was not prepared for the joy that has come from a Spring Harvest 'regular' like Lyndon Bowring, Chairman of CARE. His influence on me has been significant, and it extends even to the way many of these sermons were developed. I wish to dedicate this volume most affectionately to Lyndon.

I give thanks to Kingsway for graciously publishing this book. My deeper debt as always is to my wife Louise who often sat through these Bible Readings twice a day!

R.T. KENDALL
London
November 1989

P.S. The photograph on the back brings back memories of the morning when I was surprised with a gift from the Spring Harvest committee of a lovely blue jumper. Over the years I had always dressed as I do in my own pulpit—the only one to wear a three-piece suit. The question that day at Spring Harvest was would I actually wear it to the next meeting? I did, and the rest of the staff wore suits and ties!

PART ONE

THIS IS YOUR GOD

(He Who Justifies)

Chapter 1

The God of the Bible

ROMANS 1:16–20

I can only give a preview of Romans 1–8 and hope that you will want to examine this book. Perhaps you have always felt a little intimidated by the Epistle to the Romans. Back in 1516 Martyn Luther said, 'The epistle to the Romans is the chief part of the New Testament and the very purest gospel.' William Tyndale in 1534 called the Epistle to the Romans the principal and most excellent part of the New Testament and regarded it as an introduction to the Old Testament, so that if you understand Romans you have an advanced start on the Old Testament. Samuel Taylor Coleridge simply said, 'It is the profoundest piece of writing in existence.'

Now let me give very briefly certain pertinent facts concerning the background of the epistle. It was written in 57 AD by Paul when he was actually in Corinth. It is important to remember that the church in Rome was not founded by Paul. He had never been to Rome at the time he wrote the epistle. He envisaged going to Spain and thought that on his way to Spain he would come through Rome, and he wanted to write to them and let them know what he believed before he arrived. An interesting thing about the apostle Paul is this (something often forgotten): his first love was pioneer evangelism. He says so at the end of the epistle: 'I want to preach the gospel where Christ was never named, lest I build upon another man's foundation' (15:20). Most ministers today want to go where there is a foundation and they want to build the superstructure. Not Paul. He literally wanted to go where the name of Jesus had not even been heard. But he knew that this would not be possible when he came to Rome. Here there was a church already in existence and so what he wanted to do was to let them know what he believed.

The church in Rome was probably started by Jewish Christians who were in Jerusalem on the day of Pentecost. Because of their conversion on that day when they went back to Rome they began a church. So it was not founded by one of the twelve apostles; it was more like what we would call a house-church.

This church may well have lacked certain structure and leadership, and this is probably the best explanation for why Paul wrote as he did. Certainly no other epistle of Paul gives such a complete statement of the gospel. When he wrote to the Galatians or the Ephesians, for instance, he didn't need to say everything he believed. They already knew it. What he says in the Epistle to the Romans is what he had said in person when he wrote the other letters. But having never been to Rome, knowing he was going to come through there, he wanted them to know what he believed and so he put it all down on paper. He took nothing for granted when he wrote this epistle, whether it was the content of the gospel or even the salvation of those that he addressed. Sometimes he talks to them as believers, but then he turns around and warns them as he does in chapter 2.

Now the theme in Romans 1 is the God of the Bible. What Paul does is to confront us with the true God. In the last century the German philosopher Feuerbach said that God was nothing more than man's projection upon the backdrop of the universe. And so he dismissed the idea of God and said that God is what man dreams of God being; we put upon the backdrop of the universe the kind God who will give us pie in the sky by and by, and it keeps us going to know that a God like that exists.

In stark contrast, the God of the Bible as he emerges in this Epistle to the Romans is not the God man would want. Man would not have dreamed up this God. This is the God man abhors as a natural enemy. Hence, of course, the need for reconciliation.

The difficulty with so much theological thinking today is that it is sentimental. Sentimental talk about God *is* man's projection upon the backdrop of the universe. So that when man by nature wants to talk about God he envisages the kind of God that makes him feel comfortable. And it is always a God who wouldn't harm a flea. The sad result is that, when the true God is brought before the eyes of man, man's instinctive reaction is to hate that God. The true God makes man angry.

The true God arouses hostility in man; he shakes his fist at God. A good hint as to whether we are really witnessing properly is whether, when some hear about our God, they don't like him, they shake their fists at him. The difficulty is, because we've known men to have that kind of reaction, we tend to want to make God come out looking a little better. We want to say to people, 'But wait a minute, you need to know that God isn't all that bad!' But as Luther put it, 'You must know God as an enemy before you can know him as a friend.' Now there are two ways of doing theology. One is from man's point of view, and that is what I fear we know so much about today. And the other is from God's point of view, and that is what you have in the Epistle to the Romans.

Paul is unashamed of the God of the Bible. He's unashamed of the gospel (1:16). 'For therein is the righteousness of God revealed from faith to faith: as it is written, The just shall live by faith. For the wrath of God is revealed from heaven against all ungodliness and unrighteousness of men, who hold the truth in unrighteousness' (1:17–18). The only thing that will make us unashamed of the gospel is that we are unashamed of

God. Weak shallow superficial Christianity breeds in us the fear of man and the need to apologise for the God of the Bible. Not so the apostle Paul.

Does this surprise you? Could it be that your fear of man is to be explained by the fact that you've not really been confronted by the God of the Bible? And perhaps your unwillingness to witness for Jesus Christ wherever you are is because you haven't really been confronted by the God of the Bible. If you haven't been confronted by the God of the Bible you haven't been converted. You are still in your sins and under his wrath.

Now what is it that Paul says about the God of the Bible? There are six things I want us to see in this first Bible reading.

The God who reveals himself

'Because that which may be known of God is manifest in them for God hath showed it unto them' (1:19). He is the God who has revealed himself and does so as a God of righteousness, 'for therein is the righteousness of God revealed from faith to faith' (verse 17). So the very first things that the apostle Paul said about the true God is that his righteousness is revealed. The Greek word also means justice, and can be translated either 'justice' or 'righteousness'. But having said that, Paul straight away brings us face to face with God's wrath: 'For the wrath of God is revealed from heaven against all ungodliness and unrighteousness of men who hold the truth in righteousness' (1:18).

And then he is seen as the God who has made us: 'For the invisible things of him from the creation of the world are clearly seen, being understood by the things that are made, even his eternal power and Godhead, so that they are without excuse' (1:20).

Next Paul shows us that he is the God who has revealed himself as one who hates sin: 'Because when they knew God they glorified him not as God, neither were thankful, but became vain in their imaginations and their foolish heart was darkened' (verse 21). And the consequence, says Paul, was that God just 'gave them up'. He didn't say that he pushed them. There were no bright flashing lights in the sky. God just gave them up to the: 'uncleanness through the lusts of their own hearts, to dishonour their own bodies between themselves' (verse 24). And so that is what Paul has said so far about the God of the Bible. He's the God who reveals himself.

The God who saves

But the second thing he says is that he is the God who saves people. The gospel of Christ is 'the power of God unto salvation to everyone that believeth, to the Jew first, then also to the Greek' (1:16). So this salvation of God is the combination of two things: first, that Jesus Christ has been declared to be the Son of God through the resurrection of the dead and secondly by faith in him. We will look in Chapter 2 at the doctrine of justification by faith alone. He is the God who saves people through these two things—by his Son, and by faith in his Son.

The God who punishes sin

No question he does it—the question is how. Paul gives three ways whereby this is done. The first example is by letting men sin. He says in verse 24: 'God gave them up to their uncleanness to the lust of their own hearts to dishonour their own bodies between themselves.' Perhaps you have never seen committing sin as punishment for sin. You thought that you were getting away with it. You thought that you were outwitting God. You thought, here he is trying to reach you, while you just say, 'I'll show him. I'll just enjoy living in sin.'

But what Paul is saying here is that God has already

begun to punish you. It is a judgement of God that you remain in sin. When you think that you're getting away with it, that's the worst thing of all that can happen. The worst sign of God's judgement is that you're able to sin and get away with it. The marvel about the man of the name of Jonah is that he wanted to run from God, but he found that God went after him. And Jonah was found out. The worst thing that can happen to someone is not to be discovered.

Nor does God give us a bold sign, telling us, 'Here's what I'm going to do.' He just gives us up. He doesn't push us, he doesn't hammer us. It is a judgement of God that we can wallow in the folly of our sin. In effect Paul is saying this: is it sin that you want? Sin you will get. That's the first way God punishes sin.

The second way is by exposure at the final judgement. Say you decide to live in sin; you're thinking at first that something's going to happen as a kind of warning from God, like thunder and lightning, but when it doesn't come you think: I don't feel a thing, I'm able to go right on and do this. It's just as when Samson revealed the secret of his strength to Delilah, he 'wist not that the Lord was departed from him' (Judg 16:20). When a person does what is not right, he may say, 'I don't feel any different; I feel fine.' But how does God punish? By exposure at the final judgement. And so Paul says, 'But after the hardness and impenitent heart treasures up unto thyself wrath against the day of wrath and revelation of the righteous judgement of God who will render to every man according to his deeds' (2:5–6). And in verse 16 he refers to 'the day when God shall judge the secrets of men by Jesus Christ according to my gospel'. God can wait. He has patience and time is on his side. The day will come when the sea will give up her dead and all men shall stand before him. We are told what follows the judgement (and here's an awful word) is perishing. Verses 11 and 12: 'There is no respect of persons with God, for as many who have sinned without the law shall also perish without the law.'

Now there is something you ought to know about the Greek word translated 'perishing'. It doesn't mean extinction, or annihilation, as the cults would have us believe. The Bible shows clearly that we have been made in the image of God. I want you to think about this for a moment. We are made in the image of God, and the Bible says that God alone has immortality. This means that God can never die, and when God made us in his image it means that by virtue of our creation we can never die. Do you want to know why hell is eternal? Do you want to know why it is an everlasting punishment? It is because man has been made in the image of God. Immortality is not the gift of regeneration but creation, and this is why punishment is eternal. And when the God of the Bible is preached and we bring men face to face with what God really is, you can see that it's something that man would never have thought of. Who would have come up with a God like that? What man would want him?

One July afternoon in Enfield, Connecticut, in 1741 Jonathan Edwards preached a sermon that he later gave the title 'Sinners in the Hand of an Angry God'. Taking his text from a short verse in Deuteronomy 'Their feet shall slide in due time,' he put before men a picture of hell, and God so blessed that message that we're told that before the day was over men—strong men—were seen inside the church holding on to church pews to keep from falling into hell, while those outside were holding on to tree trunks to keep from sliding into hell. And that was what gave birth to what is known as the Great Awakening. God owned the preaching of who he is.

How does God punish sin? First, by letting people sin. Second, by exposing them at the final judgement. A third way is that God punished his Son on the cross. Eternally speaking, there are two ways whereby God punishes sin. The fires of hell; the blood of Jesus. Let this be what lingers in your mind. These two things go together: the fires of hell; the blood of Jesus. It's not a question of whether your sin will be punished, it is the question 'how'. And may God grant you to see why the Bible talks about 'fleeing from the wrath to come'. Why do you think we have words like this? Why does Paul bother to say 'being saved from the wrath to come'? Because God punished his Son; he who knew no sin was made sin.

The God of the Old Testament

The fourth thing that the apostle Paul tells us about the God of the Bible is that he is the God of the Old Testament. As a matter of fact, this is one of the very first things that Paul says in this epistle (1:1–2).

Paul lets these people in Rome know straight away what he believes about the Old Testament. My fellow Christians, never apologise for the Old Testament. Remember that the earliest church did not have what we call the New Testament. They did not have it for many many years. What did they do then? They were forced to go into the Old Testament. That's all the early church had. And Jesus never apologised for the Old Testament. The apostle Paul never apologised for the Old Testament. Now this presupposes certain assumptions. The one assumption that we must not forget is that the Old Testament God is the God of Israel. Notice again 'For I am not ashamed of the gospel of Christ, for it is the power of God unto salvation to everyone that believeth, to the Jew first and also to the Greek' (1:16). Now, when you remember that the Epistle to the Romans was put in that context, it is a reminder to us that we will never outgrow certain theological language. There *is* what we call the language of Zion.

There has been a trend in recent years, especially in certain seminaries, to say, 'We don't need some of these

old terms—man has come of age and we can come up
with symbols, the symbolic equivalent.' But wait a
minute. God chose to reveal himself through a covenant
people. He's the one that came up with the terms 'law',
'sin', 'atonement', 'justification', and these are terms that
we must learn and which we will never outgrow. Don't
try to be emancipated from our Judeo-Christian heritage, for this was the way God chose to reveal himself.

The God who warns

The fifth thing that comes from the hand of Paul in
telling us about the God of the Bible is: He is the God
who warns: 'And thinkest thou this, O man, that judgest
them which do such things, and doest the same, that
thou shalt escape the judgment of God? Or despisest
thou the riches of his goodness and forbearance and
longsuffering; not knowing that the goodness of God
leadeth thee to repentance' (2:3–4). This is something
that's got to be said about the God of the Bible. One of
the kindest things that we can say about God is that he
warns us. Why does he warn us? It is because he cares.
When does he warn? He warns when there is still hope.
God is not mocked and he does not mock us. When God
has already decided to do something irrevocably with a
particular person, or with a nation, he goes ahead and
just does it. But when he warns, that means there is still
time to do something about it. When Jonah went march-
ing into Nineveh he had one message: forty days and
Nineveh shall be overthrown. It looked as though God
had already decided there was no hope. But when the
king of Nineveh heard the message he said, 'Well who
can tell, maybe God will change his mind.' And the king
of Nineveh was right. God would not have bothered to
send Jonah into Nineveh if there were not hope. You
see, when God destroyed Sodom and Gomorrah, as far
as I'm able to tell, he didn't even warn them. He may
have but it's not in Scripture. And when Abraham saw

the smoke ascending to heaven from Sodom and Gomorrah he raised just one question (and, by the way, this ought to be your question, it is what should make us all lower our voices when we're so sure that God couldn't do these things): Abraham said, 'Shall not the Judge of all the earth do right?' (Gen 18:25). Isaiah said, 'His ways are higher than our ways, his thoughts are higher than our thoughts' (see Is 55:9).

Whereas with Sodom and Gomorrah he just did it, if he bothers to warn us it means there is still hope. This takes me back to many years ago when I was a boy of fifteen in my home church in Kentucky. We'd been running what they call a revival in America. (People call them missions in other countries and they've got the better word.) One morning after a two-week revival (mission) the evangelist who had been invited to preach wanted to see me. He was eighty years old. Apparently he'd seen me in the congregation every night because my parents always made me go to church every time the door was open! He said he wanted to use me as an illustration in his sermon. He had three of the men of the church as well, and he was explaining that in the morning service he was going to preach on the parable of the man who did not have the wedding garment— when he didn't have it he was speechless and they bound him hand and foot and cast him into outer darkness. Now this particular evangelist was a bit of an eccentric, but an anointed man indeed. He wanted this to be acted out. At the time I didn't even know of the parable but I went along with it of course, and so at a particular moment he had me come up in front of all the people and sit in a chair. And there I was, I did not have the wedding garment and I was speechless, and he called for the three men to come out of their seats and come up to the front. They took handkerchiefs and bound my hands and my feet, and literally carried me out through the centre aisle of the church. The height of my fear just then was that some of my friends would be walking down the street and see me! But something most terrible was happening that morning.

That evangelist went ahead and gave his altar call (and I understand many went forward) and he said, 'Somebody this morning is getting their last call.' Now sometimes evangelists will say things like that to scare people and it can be a manipulative thing. But this man was eighty years old. He wasn't trying to be a sensationalist or make a name for himself, but in a very sober spirit he said, 'I am not going to dismiss this service; somebody in this congregation is getting their last call.' He turned the service back over to the pastor. People sat down, and slowly they just tiptoed out of the service. Now there was a young lady in the church called Patsy, just sixteen years of age. I knew her well, and that people were praying for her, but throughout the service she laughed and poked fun at the preacher. People were turning round and telling her to be quiet but during the actual altar call she continued in this very flippant and haughty manner. Different ones were praying that she would go forward but she didn't.

The next day, at about four o'clock in the afternoon, when I had finished my little job of delivering newspapers in the area, I came home to find my mother weeping. She said, 'Have you heard about Patsy? She's just been killed.' It seemed that while she was on her way home from school, she was coming down the road towards the corner where there was a stop sign. Some kids had turned the stop sign round so that it faced the opposite way. Someone who didn't know the area didn't know he had to stop and collided with another car, driving it right up on the sidewalk and killing Patsy instantly.

I'd heard about Patsy that morning before, and I knew what the preacher had said and, do you know, I've never got over that. And yet there God was warning. The God of the Bible warns only when there is time.

The God who leaves us without excuse

The sixth and last thing Paul says about the God of the
Bible in this section is that he is the God who leaves us
without excuse. He does this through conscience: 'For
the invisible things of him from the creation of the
world are clearly seen, being understood by the things
that are made, even his eternal power and Godhead; so
that they are without excuse' (1:20). This is further
evidence that we have been made in the image of God.
Why is it that we are not able to persist in wickedness
and feel good about it? Conscience, such that things are
clearly seen to be wrong, and we are without excuse.
This being without excuse is also seen when we judge
one another: 'wherein thou judgest another, thou con-
demnest thyself' (2:1). We all want to be the exception
to the words of Jesus in the Sermon on the Mount,
'Judge not that ye be not judged' (Mt 7:1). When we
judge another we condemn ourselves. Often what
makes us the most indignant in judging another is
where we ourselves are weakest. When we are most
critical of another, one reason we can see it so plainly
is because we see ourselves in that person, albeit
unwittingly.

I remember on one occasion I was driving up to Hyde
Park Corner and the car in front of me was going so
slowly that I thought he'd never move out. I started
honking my horn and I realised right after I did it that I
hoped he wasn't in the service a few minutes before!
You know, I was so angry I said, 'What's the matter with
that man?' Do you know that when he finally left and I
was in the same spot, the guy behind me started honking! I then realised that I was in the same situation.

Always when we judge another we condemn ourselves. But it leaves us without excuse, says Paul. And
when God says he leaves us without excuse it's also
because he has given us the gospel. So we close where we
began—the first thing that God says about himself is that

he is the God of righteousness, 'for therein is the
righteousness of God revealed from faith to faith'
(1:17), so that we are without excuse. We have the
gospel. Paul took nothing for granted when he wrote
this epistle, covering everything that had to be said
about the gospel, just in case somebody in that church
was not really converted. And I don't know everyone
reading this book. Maybe you are saved, but could it be
you're not? Don't let this week pass you by till you know
that you are saved.

Chapter 2

Justified by Faith

ROMANS 3:20–28

What the apostle Paul says in Romans chapters 3, 4 and 5 is probably the most difficult thing in the world to believe and to keep believing. It is one thing for us to believe it once and be electrified and to be thrilled, to have our world turned upside down, but quite another to keep believing it, because the devil doesn't want us to believe what is contained in these chapters. He will come alongside and tell you that it can't be true. And he appeals to our natural reasoning. He appeals to what we know to be true about ourselves, that we are sinners. If he can, he will bring us right back into bondage.

It was Martin Luther who rediscovered the Pauline doctrine of justification by faith. I won't go into a lot of detail, but I want to say just a word about Luther. I myself identify with him so much and my own personality parallels his, although I wasn't brought up in the Roman Catholic tradition. But Luther was a very conscientious person. He had a sensitive conscience and was known to go to Confession not only every day but sometimes two, three times a day, because after spending an hour confessing his sins, he would come back an hour or two later remembering there was a sin he didn't confess. And sometimes the other priests would see him coming and the confessor would say to another priest, 'Would you take him for a while, I don't want to listen to any more!' Luther was afraid that if there was one sin that had not been confessed or dealt with, he would be under God's wrath and be lost. So he lived in perpetual fear.

But during these days he was also reading the Epistle to the Romans (as well as Galatians and certain of the Psalms). And here he had a breakthrough, largely from a verse that we looked at in Chapter 1: 'For therein is the righteousness of God revealed from faith to faith: ... the just shall live by faith' (1:17). And when Luther saw that what Paul was actually saying was that faith alone pleases God and it satisfies, to use Luther's term, 'the passive justice of God', his world was changed. He in fact woke up the world by his own world being turned upside down. It has been described like a man who, in the middle of the night, was climbing up in a belfry when he slipped and fell, and in order to save his life, he grabbed the rope and began ringing the bell. Just holding on for his life he was ringing the bell at 2 o'clock in the morning, and one by one lights began to turn on all over the village wondering what was going on. And the village was awakened all because one man who had been lost was trying to save his own life.

That is what Luther was doing. He did not know that he would turn the world upside down by simply trying to save his own soul. Now the interesting thing is that Paul too rediscovered this teaching. Paul realised that Abraham saw it long before, and David saw it. It's another reminder that the early church only had the Old Testament—they did not have our New Testament. And it's a reminder also that there are certain necessary terms which we must learn. Now the Jews had a decided advantage because to them were committed the oracles of God. They already knew the language of Zion. By learning the meaning of these terms we can, as it were, catch up with the Jews and go on from there. The principal thing that we are to see now is that we are justified by the combination of two things: what Jesus

did for us; and our own faith in him. Or, to put it
another way: his faith and our faith. These two things
must come together.

Christ's faith

In Romans 1:17 the Greek clearly says 'the righteousness of God is revealed from faith to faith', and that
is how the Authorised Version renders it, unlike some
more modern versions of the Bible. Now you need to
know why Paul said 'from faith to faith' and I think it
has been a bit of a mystery to many people, which is
probably why newer versions have come along and tried
to interpret it. But we can see exactly what it means if we
look at Romans 3:22—'even the righteousness of God
which is by faith of Jesus Christ [that is the translation]
unto all and upon all them that believe: for there is no
difference.' Now the phrase 'from faith to faith' is Paul's
way of saying Christ's faith must be joined by our faith.
His faith without our faith renders salvation impossible.
Our faith without his faith would make faith a work,
which would also render salvation impossible.

Now I use the terms 'salvation' and 'justification'
interchangeably but each has its own meaning. Salvation
means being saved from God's wrath (5:9). Put simply,
you won't go to hell when you die. The word justification means that God regards us as righteous in his sight.
Now here's an important thing. The word justification is
a forensic term: it belongs in the world of the court of
law. It refers to the way God sees us, not as man sees us.
And this is why Paul could refer to Christ as one 'whom
God hath set forth to be a propitiation through faith in
his blood, to declare his righteousness for the remission
of sins that are past, through the forbearance of God'
(3:25).

Now, keep in mind that justification is a legal term. It
is the way God sees us. It is not the way we may feel
about ourselves. We may feel quite the opposite. We

may feel very conscious of sin. We may feel very unworthy, but if we can understand that justification refers
to the way God sees us because our faith is in the blood
of his Son, then it will enable us to get through difficult
times when the devil would fight us and remind us of
our sinfulness. After all, Satan has a daily computer
printout, as it were, on everything about us, and he can
point to this and that, and he knows us backwards and
forwards. But this doctrine of justification will set you
free and will give you the grounds whereby you can cast
down Satan and go on, because we're not talking about
feeling, we're talking about what is true. If you can
believe it you will be set free—and you can stay free.

Now again may I point out the use of this phrase
'righteousness of God' or 'righteousness from God'. It is
in 1:17 and now Paul uses it again in 3:22. 'Even the
righteousness of God which is by faith of Jesus Christ.'
Now the word righteousness means justice, and Paul
could speak of faith to faith being what is meant by
righteousness of God simply because we're talking about
what Christ has done and what we do by the Holy Spirit.
Now in 3:22 Paul makes three things clear. The first is
that God's righteousness is by Christ's faith. Now this
may be something that you have not grasped before,
and if you've been a Christian for many years and
haven't seen it, it will probably take you longer than for
someone who is a new Christian. A new Christian can
just believe the simplicity of God's word, and if he hasn't
been entrenched in other ways of thinking, this is a
definite advantage. When I talk about the faith of Jesus
I mean just that. Jesus as a man had faith. It was a
perfect faith, and if he did not have a perfect faith we
could never be justified, and it is most unfortunate that
modern translations have decided to interpret rather
than translate. What Paul is saying is that we are saved
because Jesus as our substitute believed perfectly for us.

God required a perfect faith, and the reason there
had to be a perfect faith is because there had to be a

perfect obedience, and it is obedience that is produced by faith. So the first thing Paul says in 3:22 is that God's righteousness is by the faith of Jesus Christ.

The second thing he says is that what Christ did is offered to everybody. Let's look at it: 'even the righteousness of God which is by faith of Jesus Christ unto all and upon all' (3:22). And so it is offered to everybody, and yet we know not everybody is saved. And this brings us to the third point. God's righteousness is conferred upon those who believe. Galatians 2:16 says exactly the same thing, lest you wonder whether this is just an unguarded comment of Paul: 'Knowing that a man is not justified by the works of the law, but by the faith of Jesus Christ, even we have believed in Jesus Christ, that we might be justified by the faith of Christ, and not by the works of the law: for by the works of the law shall no flesh be justified.'

Calvin in his understanding of this teaching put it in terms of two causes. The meritorious cause and the instrumental cause. The meritorious cause is what Jesus did for us. The instrumental cause is our own trust in what he did. And so this is Paul's point, having established in 1:17 that the righteousness of God is revealed from faith to faith, when it comes back to the expression again in Romans 3:22, rather than say from faith to faith, he says it's by the faith of Jesus Christ to all who believe. So that what Christ did for us is ratified by our trust in him.

Now why did Paul use this term 'faith of Christ'? Why not 'death of Christ'? Why not 'blood of Christ', or 'obedience of Christ'? He uses those terms as well, but he will never let us think for a moment that our faith is meritorious. What Christ did is meritorious, whereas our faith is simply the instrument. Otherwise our faith would be a work. And so to introduce this teaching of justification Paul begins by referring to faith when it really was a work, the work of Jesus Christ. It is what he did. For Christ's faith was meritorious. It is later referred to as obedience: 'For by one man's disobedience many were made sinners, so by the obedience of one shall many be made righteous' (5:19). It is always faith which produces obedience, so perfect faith produces a perfect obedience.

This is something that cannot be taken for granted, and it cannot be underestimated. It was necessary that all which Jesus Christ did was done perfectly. He had a perfect faith. John the Baptist said of Jesus that to the Son the Spirit was given without measure (see John 3:34). Also Jesus produced a perfect obedience. He said early on in the Sermon on the Mount, 'I am not come to destroy [the law] but to fulfil' (Mt 5:17). It was one of the most daring claims that Jesus could have made. For no one ever had done it. No one had ever fulfilled the law, but Jesus said he was going to do it, and he did. And it was necessary that he be a perfect sacrifice, a lamb without spot. The foundation of our justification is what Jesus Christ did, not only by his death but also by his life, and maybe this study will help us to see that we're not only saved by the blood that Jesus shed but we are saved by his very life. In fact, Paul says just that in 5:10—'For if, when we were enemies, we were reconciled to God by the death of his Son, much more, being reconciled, we shall be saved by his life.'

And yet all that Christ did and suffered for the salvation of the human race is of no value until we believe.

Our faith

Now in the Epistle to the Romans sometimes Paul will speak of being saved by Christ, and when he does that he is referring to what Calvin would call the meritorious cause. For example, 'Much more then, being now justified by his blood' (5:9), he doesn't even say faith there. He's simply showing that we are justified by what Christ did, so that we can sing with the hymn writer

My hope is built on nothing less
  Than Jesus' blood and righteousness.
I dare not trust the sweetest frame
  But wholly lean on Jesus' name.

We are saved by Christ. And yet Romans 3:22 says we
are justified by faith in his blood, so that Jesus did
everything by his life, and by his death, but it is our faith
that ratifies the atonement which he procured on the
cross.

Why was the obedience of Christ necessary? In 2:13
Paul says: 'For not the hearers of the law are just before
God, but the doers of the law shall be justified.' Now
perhaps you've run into people who don't believe in
justification by faith alone and they have built their case
on that verse. And they will come perhaps to a young
Christian and say, 'Look here, the doers of the law shall
be justified.' But legalistic people never get beyond
Romans 2:13 and they take that to mean that they will be
justified by their good works. Now why did Paul say
that? Why did Paul say that it's not he who hears but he
who does who is justified? Well it was necessary for him
to say that because it was essential that somebody,
somewhere, at some time, kept the law perfectly, sixty
seconds a minute, sixty minutes an hour, twenty-four
hours a day. Somebody somewhere at some time had to
keep the law perfectly.

That is what our Lord Jesus Christ did, every day of
his life. The bottom line: we had to have a substitute.
There had to be one who fulfilled the law, and it was
Jesus. He was our substitute by his life; he was our
substitute by his death. The words of the great Charles
Spurgeon of the last century: 'There is no Gospel apart
from these two words "substitution" and "satisfaction".'

When Jesus was on the cross and could cry out, 'It is
finished,' in that moment several hundred yards away
inside the western wall, something happened. The veil
of the temple had been hanging there for years, and

looked as though it would hang for ever, but on that Friday afternoon at about 3 o'clock it was split in two from top to bottom. Why? Because God's justice was satisfied. Satisfied because of what Jesus did. Anyone therefore who is going to be saved must abandon any hope in himself. You must see that you've got nothing that you can present to God. In the words of Toplady

> In my hand no price I bring,
> Simply to Thy cross I cling.

In the meantime Paul is establishing something else which I would think needs no great amplification here. All have sinned. He established that back in chapter 2:21–22: 'Thou therefore which teachest another, teachest thou not thyself? thou that preachest a man should not steal, dost thou steal? Thou that sayest that a man should not commit adultery, dost thou commit adultery? Thou that abhorrest idols, dost thou commit sacrilege?' And what is he saying? He's showing that the Jews have sinned. He's having to establish to a self-righteous people that they have sinned. And therefore being a Jew counts for nothing. They thought that it meant something to God. He had to answer the question, 'What, then, is the advantage of the Jew?' and his answer is that the Jew has a head start, but he has sinned. Now this was shattering to a Jew, that he, even though he's a Jew, will have to have a righteousness outside of himself. But then Paul has said Gentiles too have sinned—Romans 2:12: 'For as many as have sinned without the law shall also perish without law.' So the conclusion of the matter is chapter 3:19–20—'that every mouth may be stopped, and all the world become guilty before God. Therefore by the deeds of the law there shall no flesh be justified in his sight.'

Paul speaks of righteousness without the law when he says in verse 21, 'But now the righteousness of God without the law is manifested,' but why could he say this?

It's because the law was kept for us, and that's why he refers in verse 22 to 'the righteousness of God which is by faith of Jesus Christ unto all and upon all them that believe.' And if we don't believe we won't be saved even though Jesus did everything. And so he asks what all will be thinking by now. Every time Paul raises the question it's because he assumes you're going to ask that question, because if you're understanding him as he's going along, you're going to have a question, and so he anticipates your question and he asks it for you. Thus 3:27—'Where is boasting then?' Now maybe you'd not thought to ask that, but a Jew would. Paul says boasting is excluded. And they say, 'Oh, by what law? of works?' No, by the law of faith.

There follows at this stage an important clarification and Paul brings up a word that many find difficult to understand. I'm going to try to make it as simple as I know how. It's the word 'imputation'. The question is, what happens to the person who believes? The answer is, Christ's very own righteousness is imputed to him. Imputed means 'put to the credit of'. I can put it like this. When I transfer my trust from my good works to what Jesus did for me, then God transfers Christ's faith and righteousness to me. His righteousness is put to my credit so that I'm judged not by my works but by his righteousness. And this means that no matter how long I am a Christian I will never be more righteous in God's sight than I am the moment I first believed.

And if I am a Christian for fifty years, no matter how much I have laboured, worked, walked in the light, suffered, resisted the devil, resisted sin, resisted the flesh, I will never outgrow the righteousness of Christ. I will find that I am no more righteous fifty years later because the righteousness of Christ can never be improved. It can never get better. That is the way I will be judged. And this is why the hymn writers will use the expression, 'being clothed with his righteousness'. Zinzendorf's great hymn (translated by John Wesley)

'Jesus thy Blood and Righteousness' exults in the way God sees us. He declares us to be just. He declares us to be righteous, holy, righteous as his own Son, as though we had never sinned.

What about my sins? They're forgiven. They're blotted out, all of them. And so to establish this point, Paul brings in two Old Testament examples: Abraham and David, two undisputed examples, whom all the Jews would have to accept as valid cases. Paul has said a very daring thing in Romans 4:5—'But to him that worketh not, but believeth on him that justifieth the ungodly, his faith is counted for righteousness.' It's almost as though Paul wants to stick the knife in. He says, 'I mean *ungodly* people are justified.' And people would answer that surely they must be prepared and led into it, and after a while they reach a certain stage and prove themselves, then God will say I think you're going to turn out all right, and I'll stamp 'righteous' in your case. But Paul says, 'Just a minute, what about Abraham? What kind of background did he have?' Every Jew knew what kind of background Abraham had. He was a sun worshipper, an idolater of the most extreme kind. And once Abraham was looking out at the sky on a clear night, and God came alongside and said, 'Abraham, look up.' He looked up and God said, 'Count the stars. So shall your seed be.'

At the time Abraham didn't have a child. He had no heir, and his wife was getting older. But when God said that, Abraham believed it and God said 'righteous'. 'Abraham believed God and it was counted unto him for righteousness' (Rom 4:3). Now Paul goes a step further and asks when Abraham was credited with righteousness, making the point that it was before his circumcision (4:10). And there's the proof, that Christ justifies the ungodly.

If as you read this you are aware that you are not saved, you know you've sinned and you know that you've got no bargaining power whatever, you can be converted right now and be just as righteous as any Christian, because the same righteousness that was put to their credit can be put to your credit in this very moment. Your faith is God's channel by which his righteousness is imputed to you.

Paul uses another example: David. He quotes from Psalm 32:6–7—'David also describeth the blessedness of the man, unto whom God imputeth righteousness without works, Saying, Blessed are they whose iniquities are forgiven, and whose sins are covered. Blessed is the man to whom the Lord will not impute sin' (Rom 4:6–8).

It's interesting: with regard to Abraham it was imputation of righteousness. With regard to David, it's seen from the other direction: imputation of no sin. But it comes to exactly the same thing. And Paul is saying to these Jews, I'm not saying anything new. They say Luther discovered the doctrine—no—he rediscovered it. They say Paul discovered it—no—he rediscovered it. It goes back to David, it goes back to Abraham. Why must it be like this? It's simply because God looked to and fro upon the earth and could find no one that was sinless. We've all sinned. Let every mouth be stopped right now. You have sinned; has your mouth been stopped? All the world is guilty, and this is why God sent his Son, called the second Man, the last Adam, to do what was undone by our first parent.

In Chapter 1 I quoted Jonathan Edwards. Have you ever heard of David Brainard? Had David Brainard lived he would have become Jonathan Edward's son-in-law. He was an unusual man; he was a missionary to the Indians in the state of New York and became almost a model for missionaries. After David Brainard died, Edwards published Brainard's journal and that journal is said to have been responsible for putting more people on the mission field than any other piece of literature. When John Wesley read it he wanted all ministers to read the life and diary of David Brainard.

Once David Brainard had a quarrel with God. And

the more he discovered about God the angrier he got. Brainard saw four things about God as he read the Bible, and they all made him mad at God.

The first thing he saw was that God demanded a perfect righteousness, and he knew he didn't have it. And it meant that he would have to have a substitute. He couldn't bear the thought that he would need a substitute and he kept thinking that he could do it alone, until he saw that he couldn't produce the righteousness that God required.

The second thing David Brainard saw was that God demanded a perfect faith, and once again he knew he couldn't produce it. He would try to believe perfectly, but he'd find himself doubting. And he became frustrated and got angry with God.

The third thing Brainard found out was that God could give faith or withhold it, and be just either way.

And the fourth thing Brainard discovered was that God could save him or damn him and be just either way. And at last he saw that he needed God's mercy. Rather than being angry with God, thinking that he could snap his finger and God would jump, he began to cry out for mercy. And God saved him.

Seeing the God of the Bible makes us realise that we don't have bargaining power. We've got no leverage. We've got no claim that we can make. We come before God and ask for mercy. Let me put it to you by way of an illustration. Some years ago my wife and I were driving in Miami Beach, Florida. I don't know whether you have ever been to Miami Beach. You see some advertisements in airlines where they show the hotels along there. All these hotels are on a street called Collins Avenue. My wife and I were driving down Collins Avenue and enjoying the sight. I never cease to be amazed at the luxury and splendour of those hotels. And driving down Collins Avenue, doing about thirty-five miles an hour, in front of the famous Fountainbleu Hotel, I noticed we were coming to a traffic light. It was green, but then turned yellow and red so fast that, as we were doing thirty-five miles per hour, we just went on through.

I looked in my mirror and I saw a flashing blue light. I pulled in, got out of the car and walked back, ready to play the innocent act—'What have I done wrong?' The door was open and the policeman just sat there in the car looking at me. And I knew that he knew that I knew what I'd done! He said to me, 'You went right through that light.'

I said, 'Yes I did. I hope you won't give me a ticket.'

He said, 'Why?'

I said, 'I'd appreciate it!'

He said, 'You know, I've been out here all day and I've given out nineteen tickets and I want to give out twenty so I can go home! You just went right through that light. Give me one good reason why I shouldn't give you a ticket.'

I said, 'Well I will say this: I believe in Fort Lauderdale when the lights turn yellow they say they stay yellow just a little longer. This red light turned red so fast, and we were going thirty-five miles per hour.'

He said, 'The speed limit is twenty-five!' Now he could arrest me for something he hadn't stopped me for. He repeated, 'Give me one reason why I shouldn't give you a ticket.'

I said, 'No reason, I'm just asking for mercy.'

He let me go. But I've never forgotten how I felt.

This is the way we come before God. We have no case. Just as with my traffic offence, the more we argue the more we realise just how much guilt there is. It is not great faith that God requires of us, it is simply trust in a great Saviour.

Chapter 3

Alive to God

ROMANS 6:1–6

If I did my job well in Chapter 2, you would have asked the question that Paul asks in Romans 6:1 'What shall we say then? Shall we continue in sin, that grace may abound?' If I did my job well you were anxious to know, well then, if we are saved by the righteousness of another, if it is true that if we've been converted and walk in the light for fifty years, we will never be more righteous in the sight of God fifty years later than we were when we were first converted, then, does it mean we can live as we please, we can live in sin, it doesn't matter? Well now, until you ask that question you haven't understood Paul's teaching on justification by faith. Now the Pauline teaching is always vulnerable to the charge of Antinomianism. That's a big word—it comes from two Greek words—*anti*, meaning against, *nomos* meaning law. The idea being that if you are saved by grace alone through faith and you are justified by trust in what Jesus did for you, well, it doesn't matter how you live. If you are justified without works, it doesn't matter how you live. This would be Antinomianism. Paul was accused of this. He says so back in chapter 2:8. Martin Luther was accused of this. The Council of Trent in 1545 was brought into being to deal with what they regarded as the Lutheran heresy. They contended he was teaching that if you are saved by faith alone it doesn't matter what you do or how we live.

I don't know whether you've read Dr Lloyd-Jones's books on Romans. I, by the way, recommend them unconditionally and categorically, and it may be that the most insightful comment he made was when he said (and he said it a number of times in the volumes) 'If our gospel hasn't been accused of being antinomian we haven't preached the gospel.' Paul was accused of it and Luther was accused of it. And this is why Paul raised the question. Now as we have said, if you are understanding Paul as you read him, you're going to have questions. And if you're really into Paul's skin you'll have the very question in your mind that he goes ahead and asks. He always asks the question that he anticipates you're thinking.

So he's said two things that he has to answer: the first is, if we are saved by faith alone, justified without works, then how shall we live? And the second question he has to deal with: why was the law brought in? So in chapter six he answers the question: how are we to live the Christian life? Chapter seven he answers the question: why the law? Well now, it is equally true that if you ask the question: shall we continue in sin that grace may abound? you still haven't understood Paul. Now it would seem that I'm speaking in circles but I will say it. If you don't ask: why should we live a holy life? you haven't understood him. And yet, if you ask, shall we continue in sin that grace may abound? you haven't understood him. Why? Because you should know the answer. In the words of Calvin, 'No one can put on the righteousness of Christ without regeneration.' And by regeneration Calvin actually meant not only being born again but having been given repentance.

Now the word repentance comes from the Greek word *metanoia* which means 'change of mind'. And it is something that God gives, as we saw in Romans 2:4 'The goodness of God leadeth thee to repentance.' Now why is this true? Well, because not only is faith the gift of God, repentance is the gift of God. Earlier I quoted Calvin dealing with two rather heavy concepts. For the theologically minded this would come as a great breakthrough. He dealt with two causes: what he called the meritorious cause of our justification, which is what Christ has done; and the instrumental cause, our faith. Faith is an instrument by which we see what Christ has done. We can take no credit for it. The fact that you are able to see this book right now is simply because the sun is out or lights are on. You can take no credit for it, you can just see. And that's what faith is. It is what Christ has done that matters. The fact that you can see it is faith— the instrumental cause.

The work of the Spirit

But now he brings in a third cause. And it is equally important. He calls it the 'efficient' cause, namely the Holy Spirit. Why is it we are able to see what Christ has done for us? It is the work of the Holy Spirit. Now it's very interesting that at the beginning of chapter five the apostle Paul comes as it were down to earth again. He's been bringing us these heavenly concepts and for many of us they are difficult to grasp. And perhaps you found the last chapter something that you need to work through, because Romans 3 and 4 are not easy to grasp, and at the end of this section, beginning in fact with Romans 5:3 Paul pauses, and ceases to be theological, but comes right into the real world (if I may put it like that) and says 'We glory in tribulations also'. Now this seems to be an abrupt change from having talked about imputation, being justified etc. And he says 'we glory in tribulations also: knowing that tribulation worketh patience; and patience, experience; and experience, hope.' And he says, 'I said all of that to say this, "Hope maketh not ashamed; because the love of God is shed abroad in our hearts by the Holy Ghost which is given unto us"' (Rom 6:4, 5).

At the end of the day the only way that you will believe all that Paul has been saying in an undoubted manner, is that the Holy Spirit has been shed abroad in your heart, so that you are able to see all of this, and you see it from your heart as clearly as you can see me because the lights are on. The Spirit has brought to life the glory, the power, the efficacy of what Jesus has done for us, and when you see this you'll never be the same again. You could conquer a thousand worlds. Not because intellectually you've worked through it, however important that may be, but because the Spirit has come and you're able to see it, and your world is turned upside down.

Maybe you think the only thing you need to do is to work it out intellectually (and that has its place because you need to understand it) but at the end of the day, even though you work it out intellectually, and you say, 'Ah, I see now what Paul's saying'; that is not enough. Do you believe it? And is it yours? And is it your own experience? This is something that needs to happen to every Christian sooner or later.

If God is bringing you tribulation; if you're going through some kind of a crisis at the moment and you are simultaneously struggling with the question, 'Am I really the Lord's own?' it may be that this tribulation will bring you right through to the point where you're able to see all of this, because the love of God will be shed in your heart by the Spirit in this powerful manner.

Many years ago, one day in October 1955, I was driving in my car from a little town in Tennessee on my way to Nashville. At the time I was a pastor of a church and I was a student at a college in Nashville. For days I had been going through a crisis, and I didn't understand what was taking place in my life. All I knew is that I was in a kind of continual agony. That morning I began listening to my radio in the car and I decided to turn it off and spend the rest of the time in prayer. I had an hour-and-a-half drive. I didn't have a clue that on that morning my life would be changed. I cannot give you all the details, but I want to say this: in those moments, suddenly—quite unexpectedly—I was carried right up into the heavenlies, and when I get back to heaven I'm going to ask to see a video replay of all of that, as I want to know how I was able to drive for the next hour. I mean: going through little villages in Tennessee and going through cities, I don't know how I did it. I just know this, the Spirit began to apply two verses to my heart. One was: 'casting all your care upon him; for he careth for you' (1 Pet 5:7). The other was: 'my yoke is easy, and my burden is light' (Mt 11:30). And I thought, my, I don't feel like this. My yoke is not easy, my burden is not light, and I am in such heaviness. And I began to agonise, and I thought that God was a thousand miles away, when suddenly I was aware that the Lord Jesus Christ was literally at God's right hand, interceding for me with all his strength.

It was as though he was saying to the Father, 'Either come to R T's rescue or I quit.' I never dreamed that the Lord cared so much for me. I burst into tears and I basked in glory, and in those moments over the next ninety minutes I was given a peace beyond anything that I'd ever known. I entered into a rest of soul which went beyond anything that I thought was possible in this life. I can only say that for days the person of Jesus was more real to me than anybody I would talk to. More real to me than my own existence, and I knew that what Jesus had done for me on the cross saved me for ever. I knew that I was saved and that I could never be lost. I didn't know it was possible to know this, and I was never to be the same again.

You may grasp intellectually Paul's doctrine of justification by faith, but something needs to happen to you. And this is why Paul pauses and leaves legal terms, as it were, intellectual terms, and he talks about tribulation, patience, experience and the Spirit making all of this real. And so it is all because the God of the Bible will want to reproduce himself in us. He doesn't save us to leave us in our sins. Leaving us in our sins (as we saw in Chapter 1) would be a sign of God's wrath and his punishment. Leaving us in our sins would be doing us no favour, and so the goodness of God leads us to a change of mind and a change of life. Sanctification simply understood is the process by which we are made holy. It is becoming more and more like the Lord Jesus Christ. In Romans 8:29 Paul says, 'Whom he did fore-know, he also did predestinate to be conformed to the image of his Son, that he might be the firstborn among many brethren.' When we are glorified we will be just like Jesus. We shall see him as he is. But the process between conversion and when we're glorified is called sanctification. It is the inevitable consequence of con-version. However, it is by degrees, it is imperfect in this life. But simply put, sanctification is the fervent desire to do God's will.

Dead to sin

Paul raises the question that we were all thinking: shall we continue in sin that grace may abound? He chooses to take his argument from baptism, and he puts it like this: 'Know ye not, that so many of us as were baptised into Jesus Christ were baptised into his death?' (Rom 6:3). So his argument is this: we were buried with Christ through baptism in order that we may live a new life. As Christ died, was buried, and then was raised from the dead, so we died, we are buried in baptism that we may walk in newness of life. Now Paul realises that he may be saying something to these Christians in Rome that they hadn't got before, and it may be that this teaching of justification by faith is new to you. You know that you've been converted and you know that your life has changed, and now you've discovered all that happened to you. Sometimes I think the Christian life can be described simply as a lifetime by which we're learning more and more what happens when we are saved.

Now Paul says, you decided to be baptised, didn't you? When you made the decision to be baptised, it was then, was it not, a decision to walk in newness of life? You knew this from the beginning. It follows that any clarification concerning the doctrine of justification by faith should not change your desire to please the Lord. The knowledge of it should motivate you a thousand times more. And yet he is aware that this is a very dangerous teaching. And I think a lot of ministers (and I include myself) sometimes are almost afraid for new Christians to discover this teaching. We're afraid of what it might do if they find out (and they really are saved). You've got to make a decision; do you withhold from them what is true and what will be a blessing to them, or do you let them have it, and risk them abusing the teaching?

Well now, Paul doesn't hesitate to answer that question. He says, they must be taught it. They must be taught it because any sanctification will not be what God wants it to be if the reason you live a holy life is because not living it means you forfeit going to heaven, for then that holiness of life is selfishly motivated. And the proof that you really have been saved is when you discover that you are eternally saved but now you want more than ever to glorify the Lord Jesus Christ. This is the effect it should have. And Paul wants you to know what is true about you.

I remember years ago when I had quite an argument with my father. I wasn't brought up to believe what I now preach and when I discovered it I thought I'd discovered something new. I mean, what happened to me on 31st October 1955 brought me into teaching that I thought no one had seen since the apostle Paul! Do you know, I went home and I said to my father:

'Dad, I can't wait to tell you what's happened to me.' And I told him what happened to me.

He said, 'Well, that's great, that's great.'

And then I said, 'Well, let me tell you what else

the Lord has shown me in the Bible.' I said, 'Dad, I'm eternally saved.'

He said, 'Well, very good son, very good!'

I said, 'Dad, you didn't hear me. I'm saved, I'm eternally saved.'

He said, 'Very good, very good.'

It didn't do anything for him. And it was the first pressure of real persecution from my own father. But years later I put this question to him, in an unguarded moment, when I just wanted him to answer me.

I said, 'Suppose Dad, that Michael the Archangel came down from heaven and told you that you are eternally saved?'

He said, 'Well now that would be wonderful.'

I said, 'Well supposing that happened, how would it affect you? Would you then want to live as you please and just go out and sin?'

He said, 'Oh no. I'll be honest with you son, I believe I'd want to be more godly than ever.'

I said, 'Well now, can I just say to you it's not Michael the Archangel that has told me that I'm saved, it's the Holy Spirit.'

And that's the effect that it has had on me.

Paul now shows that it is unthinkable that those who have been saved could continue in sin, and he uses an expression—it's another difficult one to grasp. He says 'Your old man has died.' Romans 6:6 'Knowing this, that our old man is crucified with him, that the body of sin might be destroyed, that henceforth we should not serve sin.' Now the point to remember is the 'old man' has died. And our old man having died is Paul's way of describing the nature of conversion. It is a transfer from one realm to another.

So faith is a transfer of trust from ourselves to Christ. God transfers the righteousness of Christ to us. But something else has happened. We have been transferred from one realm to another, from the dominion of death to the dominion of life. From the dominion of sin to the dominion of righteousness. Romans 6:9 'Knowing that Christ being raised from the dead dieth no more, death hath no more dominion over him.'

Now this concept of Paul's—the crucifixion of the old man—is not to be seen as the conscious experience. This is where a lot of people miss the point. They say, well I don't feel that this has happened to me. But you see, God says that it has happened; it's not that you feel it, it is what God says has happened to those that are in Christ. Just as the term 'justification' is a legal one—it is something that happens outside ourselves—so the crucifixion of the old man is not something we feel, it is what God says has happened, and the proof of this is in Romans 6:11. He says 'Likewise reckon ye also yourselves to be dead indeed unto sin, but alive unto God through Jesus Christ our Lord.' The NIV translates it 'Count yourselves dead'. Now this is very interesting. Why would Paul have to put it like that? Why does he say, 'Count yourselves dead', 'Reckon yourselves dead'. Well, you may not feel that you are, and the reason you have to say that to yourself is because many times you feel the opposite, but Paul says that this is what has happened, this is what is true. You are alive, you are no longer dead. This is your new identity. It's what God has said. Believe it. You are alive, as he said in Romans 8:10 'The Spirit is life because of righteousness.' The justice of God has been satisfied; you are set free. But this freedom has a corresponding responsibility. Romans 6:12 'Let not sin therefore reign in your mortal body, that ye should obey it in the lusts thereof.'

Now, note this word *therefore*. Paul loves to use this word. Probably the most important three therefores are Romans 5:1, Romans 8:1 and Romans 12:1. But Romans 6:12 does not come at the beginning of a chapter—it is not likely to get noticed—but it is of crucial importance. In the light of this glorious transference from the kingdom of death to the kingdom of light, how are we supposed to live? Romans 6:12 'Let not sin therefore reign in your mortal body, that ye should obey it in the lust thereof.' In a word, sanctification is our responsibility. It is inevitable, yes, ultimately God will see to that. But at this juncture the Lord puts us on our honour. There are no threats of chastening at this point, Paul will bring that in later, but at this point he puts it like this, 'Neither yield ye your members as instruments of unrighteousness unto sin: but yield yourselves unto God, as those that are alive from the dead, and your members as instruments of righteousness unto God' (Rom 6:13).

And here is your promise—it's in verse 14—'Sin shall not have dominion over you: for ye are not under the law, but under grace.' Never say, I can't resist sin, because you can. Never say, I can't resist temptation. Paul says you can—sin shall not have dominion over you. You may have to fight, you may have to struggle, you may have to weep, but you can say no to sin. How is this possible? Paul says there is an explanation for it. Romans 6:14 (latter part) 'Ye are not under the law, but under grace'.

Now I'm going to show you something that to me is so thrilling, so interesting, and some find almost incredible. You see, there are two ways by which one may motivate another to morality. The one is by bringing in the law. And why do some bring in the law? Well they look at it as a safety measure. 'They just feel safe so we'll give them law.' We say, look at our young people today, let's bring in the law. Paul could have withheld this teaching from the Christians in Rome if he'd wanted to. They probably hadn't heard it like this before, but Paul says they needed to know this teaching if they were to discover what holiness really is. They needed to see that the law has to be taken away. Paul says that the reason sin will not have dominion over you is because you are not under law, you are under grace. For the law, to the apostle Paul, rather than being an agent to sanctification was an impediment. It is precisely because we are not under the law that our hearts are set free to holiness. So he says in verse 22 'Being made free from sin, and become servants to God, ye have your fruit unto holiness, and the end everlasting life.'

Not under law

We come to Paul's use of the law, and that's the reason we've got the seventh chapter of Romans. Paul's teaching is: not only are we not justified by the works of the law, neither are we sanctified by the works of the law, for the works of the law will never produce the holiness that God is after. You see, the works of the law will at best produce a legalistic righteousness. Now to some that's good, fine. But that's what the Pharisees had, and the Pharisees are the ones that wanted to crucify Jesus.

I always come away from Israel utterly amazed at the blindness of the people. I don't know whether you've lived in Israel or stayed in a Jewish hotel where they're orthodox. They can bomb West Beirut and they can run the Palestinians out of their homes, but they'll keep certain laws, thank you. There's one—did you ever know about this one?—Exodus 34:26 commands the Israelites not to cook a young goat in its mother's milk. You'll find out when you go into a Jewish hotel; they keep that. They may hate your guts but they'll keep that first. And when Shabbat comes on Saturday, or rather sundown Friday, everything comes to a standstill. On my way to church on Sunday I was warned not to go to a certain area or I would be stoned. 'Thou shalt not seethe a kid in his mother's milk.' And you see when any time we bring in the law, we will always find that a particular law that we keep will give us a self-righteous feeling, like a camouflage to throw off the Holy Spirit from finding us and producing holiness in us.

And you see you can never get through to people that want to bring in the law. They will always have four or five rules that are very important to them and they're safeguards to them. Never mind hating, holding grudges, a bitter tongue, gossip, that's all right—'Thou shall not seethe a kid in his mother's milk.' We always find some rule we can keep that makes us comfortable. But you see the sanctification that Paul espouses is walking in the Spirit (see below).

I want us to see, according to Paul, the purpose of the law. Three things come out in Romans 7. The first is that Paul wants to show why God brought in the law of Moses in the first place. The answer is to show what sin is by the Ten Commandments (Rom 7:7): 'What shall we say then? Is the law sin? [somebody might have thought that that was what Paul was saying] God forbid, Nay, I had not known sin, but by the law: for I had not known lust, except the law had said, Thou shalt not covet.' God brought the law in to restrain sin by fear of punishment. It's what makes you stop at a traffic light—you don't want to get caught! And it is the way holiness was motivated—by the law. You keep it under the fear of punishment. That's what happens, the law will restrain sin, yes, by fear of punishment.

But you see Paul says, wait a minute, I know all about that, but I only found that made me worse. Romans 7:10 'The commandment, which was ordained to life, I found to be unto death.' And so why did God bring in the law? To show what sin is and that sin might be restrained by fear of punishment.

The second thought is to show that we died to the law by Christ's body. Romans 7:4 'Wherefore, my brethren, ye also are become dead to the law by the body of Christ; that ye should be married to another, even to him who is raised from the dead, that we should bring forth fruit unto God.' The kind of fruit that God wants—what he is after. This was true not only with reference to our salvation, but it is true also with reference to our sanctification—holiness—the holiness that God is after— fruit unto God, which comes when we see that we are married to another.

There is a story that has been told many times, but bears repetition. There once was a very unhappily married couple. They had an unhappy marriage, largely because the husband had his ten commandments for his wife. I mean he told her what she had to do every day, and she had to keep those rules: what time to do this, what time to do that, when to have this ready. It wasn't a very happy marriage and she was never pleasing him. Always at the end of the day he would tell her that she hadn't done this and she hadn't done that, and it was a nightmare. But one day her husband died. Some time later she remarried, this time most happily. She found a husband who loved her; she didn't know anybody could be so happy. One day she was cleaning out the cabinet and came across the old rules of her first husband, and she began to read them. To her amazement she was now keeping every one of them with the new husband without even trying. She was motivated now by love.

The third reason Paul brings in this question of the law and answers it in Romans 7 is to show that the law leads to sheer frustration. Now I realise that Romans 7: 14–21 is controversial, and I don't care to get into that. I could and we could argue about it—some say it's Paul in his pre-conversion state. Some say it's Paul in his post conversion but pre-victorious life state, and others see it as Paul in his most mature state. With respect, whatever your view may be, I'm convinced that it is a description of the agony and frustration of any man or woman who puts himself or herself under the law in the living of the Christian life. For it is not the way the Christian life is to be lived. But Paul's doctrine of sanctification is summarised in these words: 'walking in the Spirit'. And so he brought in the Holy Spirit in chapter 5:5, he comes back to him now in chapter 8:3–4—'For what the law could not do, in that it was weak through the flesh, God, sending his own Son in the likeness of sinful flesh, and for sin, condemned sin in the flesh: That the righteousness of the law might be fulfilled in us, who walk not after the flesh, but after the Spirit.' And so what the law failed to do the Spirit does. And he says, by the way, that there's nothing wrong with the law, it was just weak through our flesh. So it is not a put-down of the law. What he does in Romans 7 is to put down trying to be set free by the law.

Walking in the Spirit

What is walking in the Spirit? I want us to look at verse 6 of Romans 8. It says, 'to be carnally minded is death; but to be spiritually minded is life and peace.' Here is the clue to walking in the Spirit. It is peace. If you want to know how to be on God's signal, that is, to know his will and what pleases him and what displeases him, you come into contact with the Holy Spirit network, by which you feel peace. And now I am going to talk about feelings. I mean you can feel it. You can tell whether or not the ungrieved Spirit is at work. And when you become sensitive to the voice of the Spirit, there's peace. I'll guarantee you, when you are living in that realm you are walking not after the flesh but after the Spirit and actually fulfilling the righteousness of the law. For there's no way you could have that peace and live in sin.

And there's another thing. There is no way you can have that peace when you try to live under the law. It will be frustration and it will make you self-righteous.

About five or six years ago I went through what I thought at the time was the greatest trial I'd ever have in my life. I had been ill-treated and hurt, and I had to talk to somebody. It just happened that Josef Ton was in the country—he is a Rumanian exile now living in America, a godly man. I told him what somebody had done to me and I was expecting Josef to put his arm round me and pat me on the back and say, 'It's all right, I don't blame you. I'd feel that way too.' But he looked at me and he said, 'R T, you must totally forgive them. Until you totally forgive them you will be in chains.' I can tell you right now, not one of the Ten Commandments is as difficult to keep as what he counselled me to do. But God helped me and I did it, and I couldn't believe the peace. You see, Paul will later say these things in the rest of Romans, but we're not going to get to go to the end and so I need to point out what he means now. To be spiritually minded is life and peace. This is what is needed. To appeal to the law is to give a vote of no confidence in the Spirit, and it is also a way of binding you and making you self-righteous all over again so that you will lose joy every time. It is the power of the Spirit that will reveal sin. To let the ungrieved Spirit flow through you is to produce love, joy, peace, longsuffering, gentleness, goodness, faith, meekness, and self-control. You will abominate the works of the flesh: sexual immorality, idolatry, witchcraft, hatred, jealousy, selfish ambition, envy, drunkenness, holding grudges. Now this is the holiness that God is after.

Chapter 4

A Part of the Family

ROMANS 8:28

In this chapter we come to the undoubted high water mark of the Epistle to the Romans—chapter 8. It is possibly the greatest chapter in the New Testament. It is the Mount Everest. It is rivalled in eloquence possibly only by 1 Corinthians 13 or Philippians 2:5–11.

What I want to do is to outline the chapter. It seems to me the best way to understand Romans 8 is in terms of the family—the family of God. For example in verse 14, 'For as many as are led by the Spirit of God, they are the sons of God.' And he goes on to say, 'Ye have received the Spirit of adoption, whereby we cry, Abba, Father. The Spirit itself beareth witness with our spirit, that we are the children of God: and if children, then heirs; heirs of God, and joint-heirs with Christ' (v 15–17). So in this chapter we see God as our Father, Jesus as our elder Brother, and the Holy Spirit as the One who comes alongside. He has called us into the family. Back in verse 2 is Paul's description of what we would call being born again, regeneration, 'For the law of the Spirit of life in Christ Jesus hath made me free from the law of sin and death.' And then the Spirit not only calls us into the family, but shows us the way to walk as a family, 'That the righteousness of the law might be fulfilled in us, who walk not after the flesh, but after the Spirit' (v 4).

Then we also see in verses 14 and 16 how the Spirit

communicates our status in the family, as a family. 'As many as are led by the Spirit of God, they are the sons of God . . . The Spirit itself beareth witness with our spirit, that we are the children of God.' And the Spirit also communicates our need to the Father. Look at verse 26, 'the Spirit also helpeth our infirmities [our weaknesses]: for we know not what we should pray for as we ought: but the Spirit itself maketh intercession for us with groanings which cannot be uttered.' So that is what we have in Romans 8. God is our Father; Jesus Christ is our elder Brother; the Spirit comes alongside and even communicates our need to the Father when we don't know how to pray.

I want us to see this chapter in terms of four things. First, the family spirituality. Second, the family status. Third, the family secret. And finally, the family security.

The family spirituality

In terms of the family spirituality, Paul speaks of our walking in the Spirit. As we saw in Chapter 3, this is Paul's idea of sanctification. Walking in the Spirit. As he said to the Galatians, 'Walk in the Spirit and ye shall not fulfil the lust of the flesh' (5:16), for walking in the Spirit is the guarantee of righteousness. Notice the irony of the matter of those Christians who feel that they must go back to the law, as they see the law as a kind of safety net for holiness. The irony is this: those who try to keep the law, don't. And yet those who walk in the Spirit, do. Why? It's the New Testament way. It is what Paul refers to in Ephesians as not grieving the Spirit, and so it is letting the ungrieved Spirit be himself in us (Eph 4:30). This is what God wants to do. He wants to be himself in us, and the only way that can happen is that we don't grieve his Spirit, we don't quench his Spirit, we let him be himself. We say to a person who comes to see us, 'Make yourself at home.'

But when it comes to the Holy Spirit we must

remember this about him. He is the most sensitive
person that ever was. I don't have vocabulary to convey
to you how sensitive the Holy Spirit is. Perhaps you have
known a sensitive person who would never let you know
that his feelings were hurt, he wouldn't let on at all.
You would never know it. You see the Spirit is like that,
at the time. Remember what I said about Samson. When
he gave his secret to Delilah, he didn't know what had
happened. He didn't know that the Lord had departed.
And you see the Spirit doesn't tell us when he's grieved;
no lights flash, no thunder roars. We realise only later
when we try to operate in our own strength that this is
what has happened.

The task of the Christian life is to narrow the time gap
between sin and repentance. When a person sins, often
he doesn't see it at the time. It may be our pride, we
don't want to admit that we've sinned, and sometimes it
takes days before we say, yes, I was wrong. Sometimes it
takes even years before we finally see that we sinned,
and then we say, why did I have to wait so long?
Spirituality is narrowing the time gap between sin and
repentance. It may take years, it may take weeks, but the
more spiritual we are it may take only days, or less. Far
better if it takes almost no time at all. Then we are apt to
catch ourselves and not grieve the Spirit at all and walk
in the Spirit. Again, that is the New Testament way.

So the reason that the way of the Spirit is life and
peace is not only because it will keep you out of trouble,
but you will know the Spirit's joy and his peace. But
remember that the Spirit can be grieved. And when we
get to verse 13 Paul gives one of the graver warnings to
Christians in this epistle. He says, 'For if ye live after the
flesh, ye shall die.' This is partly a reference to pre-
mature physical death. I think that this is a rather
missing note in our thinking today. It was common
knowledge in the early church and this was an assumption which we tend to forget: that it is possible to hasten
our very death by disobedience. Do you remember what

Paul had to say to the Corinthians who had partaken unworthily of the Lord's Supper? He said some of them were weak and sickly and some were asleep (1 Cor 11:30). It means that God just says if you're not going to listen to me, your time is up—come on home. This is chastening.

There are three stages of chastening: internal, external and terminal chastening. As I said in the last chapter: don't worry, God will see to it that you are holy. It is the inevitable consequence of those truly converted.

So there are three ways whereby this can be accomplished. The word 'chastening' means correction by punishment. Not for the sake of punishment, but as the writer of Hebrews put it, 'Our fathers corrected us according to their own pleasure but our Father does it for our profit' (see Heb 12:10). He has a way of chastening us, and the *internal* chastening is the best way to have this happen. That is through the word, through preaching, through listening to the Spirit, letting him correct you. Have you had times when the Holy Spirit has dealt with you and you say yes, Lord, thank you? Now that's the best way to have your problems solved.

But if that doesn't work God has a second way: *external* chastening. That's when he sends the wind, he sends Jonah's fish, he comes from outside. He has a way of putting you flat on your back. He has a way of withholding vindication. He has a way of causing financial reverse. God can do that, as a way of saying, 'Are you going to listen to me or not?'

But the advanced stage, when all else fails, is *terminal* chastening. And Paul is warning us, 'If ye live after the flesh, ye shall die: but if ye through the Spirit do mortify the deeds of the body, ye shall live' (v 13).

The family status

I come now to the family status. And what we learn is this: that we are called sons of God. Now this comes as a surprise to some. After all, is not Jesus the Son of God? As a matter of fact Jesus is God's only natural Son (if I may put it that way), for Jesus is God. He was God as though he were not man. He was man as though he were not God. He's God's only natural Son, and yet we are called sons.

In what way then are we sons? Paul tells us it is by adoption. This is how it is we are sons of God, by adoption. And what Paul goes on to say is that we are joint heirs with Christ, and this gives us a hint as to how firm our status is in the family. How much do you think that God loves his Son? Have you any idea how much God loves his Son? The voice came from heaven at Jesus' baptism, 'This is my beloved Son, in whom I am well pleased' (Mt 3:17). The voice came at the Mount of Transfiguration, 'This is my beloved Son ... hear ye him' (Mt 17:5). Jesus said in Matthew 11 that no one knows the Father but the Son and no one knows the Son but the Father (see Mt 11:27). The relationship between the Father and Son—Jesus said, 'The Son does nothing of himself but what he sees the Father do' (Jn 5:19).

How secure is Jesus' position in the Godhead! And now I read that we are joint heirs with Christ. Is there any possibility that Jesus could be disenfranchised from the Godhead? Is there any possibility that we could be disenfranchised from the family? Never! We are joint heirs with Christ by adoption.

Now I don't know how much you may happen to know about adoption. Some years ago I was given the privilege of witnessing first-hand a court hearing in Fort Lauderdale where the judge was getting ready to finalise the adoption for some parents who had taken in a child about a year before. The rule there is that you are given the child for a while and they come and see you now and then and see that everything is going all right, and finally it becomes legal. Once it's legal it is irrevocable. And so the judge looked across at that couple in the gravest manner and he said to them, 'I want you to know that before I sign my name to this document you still have an opportunity to back out of this. Once I sign my name your son has all the rights of a natural son. You don't know how he's going to turn out. He may become unwell, he may develop a disability. As a teen-ager he may turn to drugs, but if I sign my name to this document there's nothing you can do after that. It is irrevocable and he's protected by the law of this land. Are you aware of this?' The parents looked up and they said yes. He signed his name. That judge got up from his seat and walked around and congratulated the parents. He then confided: 'I too have adopted a son.'

When we were made members of the family, we were given all the rights of the natural son. We were made joint heirs with Christ and that's our status in the family. And as Paul now begins to show something of our status as Christians in Romans 8, what he's after is that we will believe that we are members of the family and never doubt God's love. I ask you who are parents, do you or do you not want your children to believe that they are yours? Do you want them to believe that you love them? Do you think it is good for them to be in some kind of doubt whether or not you love them? Do you think that this is better for them—do you think that you can get more out of them, that you can get them to produce better if you leave them in just some doubt as to where they stand? Or is it not that you want them to know more than anything that they are loved, they are cared for, and that they are loved from the heart? Isn't this what you want them to believe?

So you see why Paul is at pains to show us that we are saved by the righteousness of another, that we are not under the law. And now he says the Spirit has come and testified whereby we cry, 'Abba, Father'. He's trying to show us that God wants to convey that we are loved, that we are special and that there's no way that we can be disenfranchised. If I thought that there was the remo-test possibility of being disenfranchised from the family,

I would be in constant fear. If I were told that there would only be one person in all of the family of God that could lose his status as a child of God, I would worry all my life that I would be that person. But you see what Paul is showing now is that this God who sent his Son into the world to die on the cross for our sins has completely satisfied the justice of God. And he wants us now to enjoy this and to live in such a way that we know we're members of the family and that we are cared for, and, as a result, throws in the family secret.

The family secret

We come now to Romans 8:28—it happens to be my favourite verse in the Bible. I call it Paul's most comforting statement. 'And we know that all things work together for good to them that love God, to them who are the called according to his purpose.' It is so comforting. It's one of those verses that you need more and more the older you get. It is the verse that in fact refers not to the future but to the past. If I may use a couple of big words here—it is not *a priori*, it is *a posteriori*. *A priori* is looking forward. *A posteriori* is looking backward. And Romans 8:28 is the promise *a posteriori*—it is after the fact. It is not *a priori* because if you could say, 'Well, everything's going to work out all right, it doesn't matter what I do' then you would abuse this promise. But you see what Paul knows is that as members of the family, we all have a sense of shame over something in our past. We've all got skeletons in our cupboards, and he can say because you're members of the family and you're joint heirs with Christ, anything that happens to you has got to turn out for good. All things work together for good—all things. Was this an unguarded comment of Paul—*all* things? It was a phrase he used all the time, he knew what it meant. He said Jesus Christ was before all things, and by him all things consist. And he could say, I can do all things through Christ who strengthens me.

Now, having established our position in the family, he's saying that God knows the past, he knows what's bothering you. All things work together for good. You could almost call it the family scandal! How do you know that? Well, because it says it works together for good—it shows it wasn't good. If it had been good he wouldn't need to say it, but it works together for good because it was bad. It doesn't mean that everything that happens is good, things that can happen can be bad, but because you're in the family you've got a promise: it will work together for good.

'Well,' somebody says, 'you know, I just don't believe that.' I've actually heard people say when they read Romans 8:28, 'I don't believe that.' That's because it's the family secret. Paul says, we know. You may not, but *we* know that all things work together for good. How do we know? Well, we've found it out for one thing. Look back—look across the years—remember the closed door that broke your heart and you lived long enough to thank God a thousand times it was closed. Learn the joy of God's providence, knowing that with every disappointment—give it time—you'll be thankful for it. He will sanctify to you your deepest distress. This is something that God does. A lot of people say, 'well if everything works together for good I need to work this out now; something's happened which is very bad and I'll see what I can do to make it work together for good.' Have you ever tried this, when you think you need to make it work together for good, and you've looked at this as your promise and thought, if it's got to work together for good, you'll see what you can do? And what happened was, that as surely as you tried to make it work together for good, it got worse.

Let me tell you what happened. When God looked down and saw you trying to manipulate things, he just folded his arms and said, 'All right you try it.' And it just got worse, until finally you said, 'Lord, I'm really making a mess, I just turn it over to you.' God said, 'Are you sure? Okay just leave it to me.' God is the only one who makes everything work together for good.

Now let me give you a caution. If you see this verse as a green light to do anything you want, I need to tell you that it doesn't mean that it will work together for good by tomorrow afternoon. It may take a little time, and God may chasten you severely if you take advantage of a verse like this. Because some are in the family, they think they can't do anything wrong. One day David walked out on his balcony and stretched after a nap, and he saw in the distance a lovely woman washing herself, and he sent word to his servants asking who it was. They told him she was married, her husband was Uriah the Hittite. David asked where her husband was, and when he found out he was one of his soldiers and was in the battle, he asked for them to send the woman, and she came. What they thought would only be an afternoon affair, turned out to cause David awful trouble. She had to send word a few weeks later that she was going to have a baby. Well David probably panicked at first, but said, 'No problem.' He sent Uriah the Hittite home and gave him a weekend holiday with his wife. But he didn't know that Uriah was going to be such a sensitive person and that he wouldn't sleep with his wife. This infuriated David, and finally David put Uriah the Hittite on the front of the battle and had him killed. That's how low David sank.

And do you know what? David paid for that—he paid severely. Yet in God's purpose, if you didn't know about that, see what you read in Matthew 1—the boring begats! The reason we don't give the gospel of Matthew to a new Christian is that we don't want him to become demoralised in the first five minutes! Well, I'll show you something interesting when you first start, in verse 6: 'Jesse begat David the king, and David the king begat Solomon of her that had been the wife of Uriah' (Mt 1:6). Why mention that? It's God's way of showing that he closes the gaps. He closes ranks. All members of the family have this promise. All things work together for good.

Now is it because we're just lucky or something like that? Some people feel that because we're in the family, everything will work out okay. But there's a reason for it: 'For whom he did foreknow, he also did predestinate to be conformed to the image of his Son, that he [his Son] might be the firstborn among many brethren' (8:29). The reason that all things work together for good is because the family name is at stake, and Jesus Christ is the one by whom the whole family is named. His honour is at stake. God is determined to make every member of the family to be just like Jesus. All of us are in the process of being made more like Jesus. God may have to use terminal chastening, he may have to use external chastening, and most of us know about internal, don't we? And he's always correcting us by his word.

Someone walked up to a sculptor who had a big block of marble. He had been commissioned to make a horse, and although he was a famous sculptor, it was yet to be seen how the finished product would turn out. Someone went up to him and said, 'How can you make that big block of marble look like a horse?' He said, 'It's a very easy answer. I just chip away everything that doesn't look like a horse!' And that's what chastening is—God just chips away everything that's not like Jesus. The family name is at stake.

And then Paul throws in another word. This thrills me to bits! I don't want us to have any controversy over it, but it's this: 'Moreover whom he did predestinate, them he also called: and whom he called, them he also justified, and whom he justified, them he also glorified' (v 30). The old illustration is the best: on the front of the big gates of pearl are the words, 'Whosoever will may come,' and we walk through the gate and turn around and look on the other side of the gate and it says: 'Chosen from the foundation of the world.' And we find out that for some reason (I don't understand it, we may never understand it) God chose us from the beginning to be members of his family.

And note this, that whom he called, them he also justified, whom he justified, them he also glorified. As surely as you're justified, you know how the end will be. You see, God wants you to know how it's going to turn out. He wants you to know now. Why? It's going to make all the difference in the way you live your Christian life. You won't be trying to earn your way. And you won't have a fear of the outcome in the end. God wants you to know from the beginning that you're his—that you're loved with an everlasting love. And as surely as you're justified you know that you're going to be glorified. And how do you know that you're justified? Simply because you've transferred all trust in yourself to what Christ has done for you, and put all of your eggs into one basket— Jesus has lived and has died for me. That's how I know how it's going to be in the end. God wants to restore to the Christian church a sense of assurance, that we know how it's going to turn out, so that there's no fear of death.

Josef Ton once said to me, 'The most dangerous person in the world is someone who is not afraid to die.'. We're called to go into the world, but the pity is, that so many of us are cowards, or ashamed, afraid how it's going to turn out. But if we can know that we're members of the family and that God is going to protect the honour of his Son—and if he wants us to know that he's got a purpose, and that as far as our salvation goes, instant death is instant glory—how can we be afraid? If this sense of assurance would come back to the church, then like a mighty army we can invade Satan's territory and be a threat to Satan. It could well be that the day will come when they will be begging for us. Instead of our having to write letters to Thames Television or to Parliament, they'll come to us asking, 'What do we do now?' This can happen if we take seriously our status in the family.

The family security

I come now to the last part: the family security. Now this has been implicit all along. It's as if Paul wants to recap everything at this point. Why is it true? He's wanting us to know beyond any conceivable doubt how much God loves us, and he concludes at the end in verses 38 and 39, 'I am persuaded that neither death, nor life, nor angels, nor principalities, nor powers, nor things present, nor things to come, nor height, nor depth, nor any other creature, shall be able to separate us from the love of God, which is in Christ Jesus our Lord.' Now why is this true? He gives a trinitarian answer in Romans 8. The first reason is because the Holy Spirit prays for us. We saw it a moment ago: the Spirit helps our infirmities, our weaknesses. You have infirmities, and I have them. What may be mine may not be yours, what may be yours may not be mine. We don't like to talk about them, do we? We wear the mask and don't want others really to see us. I wear a mask, I don't want you really to know me. You may not like me if you really knew me. But you see what is said about our Lord Jesus in Hebrews 4:15 is that he is touched with the feeling of our weaknesses. I see your weakness and I might think, yuk! But the Lord is touched, and the Spirit helps our weaknesses.

When we don't know what to pray for, he prays for us. And what does he say? It would be nice if we could know—he uses groanings that cannot be uttered. Do you know what it is to pick up the telephone and be on a party line where you can hear people talking? Years ago I was the pastor of a church in Indiana. It was out in the country, and there were nine people on the party line, and you were lucky if you got to use the phone! One day I picked it up and lo and behold they were talking about me! I could take only so much and I put it down! But wouldn't it be great if we could just hear what the Holy Spirit is saying about us, and then we'd say, Lord I agree, I pray for the same thing. But the beauty is that for the whole time the Holy Spirit prays for us, he does it according to the will of the Father. In our praying we may misfire a thousand times, but the Spirit gets it right. That's what ensures how it's going to turn out.

And then Paul says that God the Father is for us.

Isn't it great when someone comes along and says, 'I'm for you'? Many years ago when I first had to break from my old denomination, my grandfather said this about me and I never forgot it. He said, 'As for what R T is doing I don't know what it is, but I'm for him right or wrong.' And that was what I needed, to be cared for. To have somebody who's just for you; you may be in the wrong but he's for you. If God be for us who can be against us? The proof: verse 32 'He that spared not his own Son, but delivered him up for us all, how shall he not with him also freely give us all things?' God's for us. He's not angry with us. His justice has been completely satisfied. The fires of hell will never satisfy the justice of God. But one drop of the blood that Jesus shed on the cross satisfied his heart. Now he can look over the family and say, 'They're mine—I've bought them.' That's how much he cares.

Paul concludes, it is because of what Christ has done and does. He says, 'Who is he that condemneth?' (v 34). Has somebody been judging you? The devil has, he's the accuser of the brethren. The devil will always come along and throw up something. He knows your past and he'll throw up something and say, 'Ah, you couldn't possibly be a Christian and have that weakness.' And Paul anticipated you might have those thoughts, so he just asks the question, 'Who is he that condemneth? It is Christ that died' (Rom 8:34). That's your assurance, not because from now on you'll be better. Not because you're going to be closer to God from now. You may have that desire and it's a good one, but if that's the basis of your assurance then your spirituality will be up and down, up and down, like a graph on a chart. As the hymn says,

> When all around my soul gives way,
>   he then is all my hope and stay.

Why? Because Christ died.

> I need no other argument,
> I need no other plea,
>   But only this: that Jesus died,
> And that he died for me.

But Paul isn't finished. He uses a very interesting word here—'also'. He said, 'It is Christ that died, yea rather that is risen again, who is even at the right hand of God, who *also* maketh intercession for us.' Now this refers to two things: not only that Jesus intercedes in addition to having died and being raised from the dead, but earlier he said that the Spirit intercedes, Now he says that Christ also intercedes. And we have seen already that a part of our Lord's work for us is that he had a perfect faith. Well now I ask, when he intercedes for me at the right hand of God, does he get his prayers through? I can tell you he does. He prays with a perfect faith, and as Paul said in Galatians 2:20—'I live by the faith of the Son of God.'

I go by the name of R T. My father named me after his favourite preacher—R T Williams—his name was Roy Tillman. Dad didn't like the name Roy so he named me Robert Tillman but he always called me R T. I was R T from the moment I was born, I mean one hour old. I've known nothing but R T all my life. Well, when we had our son I wanted to name him after me. He's Robert Tillman II, and we didn't know what to call him. Someone one day said try T R and it just stuck.

When we left the United States to come to live in England, it was a real trauma for T R. In fact during our days at Oxford he would say, 'God, thank you for the food and help Daddy to get his D Phil so we can go back to America.' We had it rough in those days at Oxford, and I'd say to the family, 'It's all right, one day we're going home.' But we woke up one morning and realised that we weren't going home. I had accepted the call to Westminster Chapel in London, and now I had to take T R to his new school in Ealing. New playground, new teachers, new friends. And we got to the school in the car and I said, 'You'll have to go, T R,' and he started to cry and said, 'I can't do it.' What I haven't told you was that he had three changes of school because we'd moved into London for six months and that was a new school, and then we had another change right after Oxford as there was a transition period. I said, 'You'll just have to go,' and he said, 'I'm not going.' I said, 'T R, look at me. I'm going to promise you right now, I'm going to be praying for you all day long. Whenever you get in a sad state just remember right then—Daddy is praying for you—whenever it happens, right then I'm praying for you.' He opened the door, got out and walked to that playground, never looking back.

He wasn't living by his faith, he was living by mine. He was living by my praying for him. So Paul could say, we live by the faith of the Son of God. And Paul could say, 'It is Christ that died, yea rather, that is risen again ... who also maketh intercession for us' (Rom 8:34). Because the God of the Bible has been satisfied by what his Son has done and still listens to his Son's praying. And we can just live by that.

God wants you to know how the end will be, and, by the way, if you were going to be dying an hour from now, this is the only thing that will give you comfort. What hope will you have in your works then? What will your promises mean then? You only have one hope.

> My hope is built on nothing less
>   than Jesus' blood and righteousness.
> I dare not trust the sweetest frame
>   but wholly lean on Jesus' Name.

And if it's good enough to die by, it's good enough to live by. And that is what Paul wanted to accomplish in the lives of those people.

PART TWO

WHERE TRUTH AND JUSTICE MEET

(Jesus: His Call and Challenge)

Chapter 5

Gathering a Family

JOHN 1

The Bible passages in this section are from four chapters of the fourth gospel, the Gospel of John. In chapter 1 we're going to see something of how Jesus was identified and how he began to gather a family around himself. Then, in chapter 6, we will see how he addressed those in the family and outside the family. In chapter 8, the whole chapter is exclusively addressed to those outside the family; but then in John 15 Jesus addresses only those within the family.

I want to put three questions before you in this second section of the book. The single most important question you'll ever have to answer is: Who is Jesus? And whatever problem you may have brought with you, this question is the one that matters. You may be under a lot of pressure, perhaps you brought it with you from home, from work, from school, from university. Perhaps there's financial pressure, perhaps you're under emotional pressure, perhaps there's a problem with relationships, perhaps you have a physical problem, or perhaps your marriage is on the rocks and nobody knows about it but you. Perhaps there's a problem you're about to have to face and yet you don't have all the data in order to make the decision. It may be at work, it may be at home. It may be that you're having terrible difficulty with a friend or with an enemy. And I still say the most important question you have to answer is: who is Jesus? For one hundred years from now that is the question that will matter, and you're not ready to deal with problems at the moment until eternal matters are dealt with.

The second most important question that you'll have to answer is this: have you met Jesus? Do you know beyond any doubt that you know him? Or do you know for sure that if you were to die today, you would go to heaven? It was on Easter morning 1941 that I came to my parents, maybe because it was Easter, and, hearing them talking about the Lord, fell under conviction and started to weep. I said, 'I want to be saved.' Obviously I'd heard language in the home which spoke of the need to be saved, and my father had the spiritual acumen not to put it off. He said, 'We don't have to wait till we get to church,' and we knelt at my parents' bedside. And that was how, on that Easter morning, Jesus came into my heart and I knew I was saved.

Now not all know the day or the hour. It's good if you do, but there are those who can't pinpoint a time. Augustus Toplady (the author of the hymn 'Rock of Ages') once said, you may know that the sun is up although you were not awake when it arose, and it's not important that you know the exact moment, but do you know that you have met him?

The third most important question you'll ever have to answer is this. Are you following Jesus? Perhaps you know vaguely who Jesus is, but you haven't met him, and perhaps you've met him but you're not following him.

Could it be that I'm addressing someone at the moment who is a fence-straddler? You've been on the fence for weeks and months, and at one moment you're looking on the God-ward side of the fence, other times at the worldly side of the fence. I pray that in the name of God you'll get off the fence on God's side even as you read this book.

Now I want to call attention to the order of these questions. Who is Jesus? Have you met him? Are you following him? Some have met him in a sense but didn't know who he was. And strange as it may seem, some follow him but don't really know who they're following. It's like those in John 6 (which we'll look at in Chapter 6) where five thousand began following Jesus. At the end of the chapter we read, 'Some walked back and went no more with him.' You see, some just follow a crowd and assume they're following Jesus. And so I ask you: Who is he? Have you met him? Do you know him?

Now in John chapter 1 there are no fewer than eight titles given to Jesus. In answer to the question, who is he, he's called the Word of God, the Lamb of God, the Son of God. He's called Rabbi, he's called Messiah, he's called Christ. He's called the King of Israel, and he's called the Son of man. There are four different sources—John the son of Zebedee, one of the twelve, who wrote the fourth gospel, called him the Word of God. John the Baptist called him the Lamb of God and the Son of God. His followers variously called him Rabbi, Messiah, King of Israel. Jesus referred to himself as the Son of man. Now the question is: how do you come to know Jesus?

Who is Jesus?

John begins the fourth gospel with the glorious revelation; Jesus is God in the flesh. It's got to be said that that is generally not the order which people come to know who Jesus is. They end up there—yes—and one must end up there, but they usually don't begin there. And that is not the order that the disciples themselves came to understand Jesus. They first saw him as a man. In fact, to put it another way, the way Jesus described himself at the very end of the chapter, as Son of man, is the initial way men are likely to see him. And so were we to invert the order of John 1 and look at it the way it ends, we would probably come closer to the order in which people come to see who Jesus is. They see him as a man, teacher, Messiah, Christ, Son of God, Lamb of God and the Creator God made flesh. But John himself, who no doubt went through these stages, at the end of the day, after the Spirit came down on the day of Pentecost, saw that this Man of Galilee whom he had followed for three years, was none other than very God of very God, very Man of very Man, so that when he began the gospel of John he simply started out with the bottom line. 'In the beginning was the Word, and the Word was with God, and the Word was God ... And the Word was made flesh ... (and we beheld his glory, the glory as of the only begotten of the Father,) full of grace and truth' (John 1:1, 14). Now that's the way John began, but then he proceeds to show the way ordinary men are led to see this. To see Jesus as God is the ultimate revelation by the Holy Spirit.

So John begins the fourth Gospel with what to him is the greatest discovery that ever was. And it's as though there's no introduction at all, he can't wait to say it. Now, as you know, the Gospel of Matthew begins with the genealogy of Jesus. The Gospel of Mark begins with the baptism of Jesus. The Gospel of Luke begins telling about the parents of John the Baptist. But John begins the gospel with the person of Jesus and says right at the beginning the greatest things that can be said about him. He refers to that than which no greater can be conceived; that the most high God who is from everlasting to everlasting was made flesh, and he says it right off, and gives the bottom line at the beginning. It's like when you are waiting to have a baby and you just want to know, is it a boy, is it a girl? And later on you find out the details, like when did the baby come along? How much did it weigh?

Many years ago, when I was twelve I was taken to Washington D C. It was a great opportunity to go to Washington and see the U S Capitol building, the

White House, the Washington Monument and the
Smithsonian Institute. But when I got back home and
my friends asked what it was like, I said, 'I saw Joe
Dimaggio the baseball player, centre fielder for the New
York Yankees.' The New York Yankees were in town,
and I got to go and see Joe Dimaggio. I actually went up
to the dugout and got within twenty feet and took his
picture. You're saying, 'You went to Washington and
you saw Joe Dimaggio!' Ah, but that's what the trip
meant to me. And maybe to some when you hear how
John began his gospel you would have thought that he
would first talk about Lazarus being raised from the
dead, or how Peter walked on the water, or how the five
thousand were fed with the loaves and the fishes.
Perhaps John would begin with the Sermon on the
Mount or describe what it was like to stand beside the
mother of Jesus at the crucifixion. You can think of all
that John could have said, or should have said, but he
began his Gospel with the single most important truth in
the world. In the beginning was the Word.

Now the 'Word' is the translation of the Greek *logos*. It
is one of those words which I think personally would've
been better left untranslated, because that way it could
take on its own meaning. To translate *logos* is very
difficult; it means faculty of thought, it means word, it
means reason. But this is one of those words which, had
the writers or translators just left it alone, it might have
taken on its own meaning, because we don't really know
what it means exactly but it is referring to a person in
the Godhead. God who had no beginning. John wants to
say that this Jesus is like that. But before he became
Jesus of Nazareth he could be called the Word who had
a trinitarian relationship from all eternity. He was with
God showing the trinitarian relationship, and he was
God. For John wants us to know that this One that he
met at the sea of Galilee went back beyond Bethlehem,
for he was in the beginning. He went back beyond the
day that Abraham discovered—'Abraham rejoiced to

see my day and was glad,' said Jesus. But John said that this Word goes back long before sin ever emerged in the Garden of Eden, long before there was ever a star or a moon, long before God let the sun shine in creation's morning. If there had been one speck of dust in remotest space, then we could not be talking about the beginning.

But John wants us to know that there was a point in time, as it were—or it may make sense to say *before* time—when there was nothing but God. And this One who was with God was God. He was a person in the Godhead, co-existent in eternity with the Father and the Spirit. Co-equal in eternity with the Father and the Spirit. But, unlike the Father and the Spirit, the *logos* was made flesh. John doesn't tell us what could be told about the birth of Jesus. He let Matthew and Luke do that. He doesn't tell us what could be told about the childhood of Jesus. He let Matthew and Luke share some of that. But he told us what is more precious to him than anything else that can be told, that the Creator God was made flesh.

As Paul put it to the Colossians, 'For by him were all things created, that are in heaven, and that are in earth, visible and invisible, whether they be thrones, or dominions, or principalities, or powers: all things were created by him, and for him: And he is before all things and by him all things consist' (Col 1:16–17).

So, says John in verse 3, 'All things were made by him: and without him was not anything made that was made.' And so we're talking now about the most fundamental truth there is. Do you believe it, that this Jesus was God as though he were not man and he was man as though he were not God? Perhaps I'm addressing someone at the moment whose problem is that you're just not sure if you're really saved. Perhaps you are like some who wish they could pinpoint a time when they know they were converted. There are those who can tell you when, and you can't. And you look at your life and you say, 'I'm not sure that I'm a Christian. There's so much about me that's wrong and not good. Surely I'm not a Christian?' Let me put this to you; do you believe that Jesus is God? Said Paul, 'No man can say that Jesus is the Lord, but by the Holy Ghost' (1 Cor 12:3). If you in your heart of hearts believe that Almighty God was made flesh and that was Jesus of Nazareth, and you testify that Jesus has come in the flesh, I put it to you today that you may know that you are saved, that you're a child of God, for none could see—*really* see—this truth but by the Holy Spirit.

Many years ago we had a pastorate in Ohio—a tiny little town about sixty miles north of Cincinatti. I took a pastorate there because they said they didn't have any doctrine but the Bible. A lot of churches in America use the little slogan: 'No book but the Bible, no law but Love, no creed but Christ.' I thought that was the greatest thing I'd ever heard, so when they called me as their pastor I accepted the call. But after a few months I began to have all kinds of problems, and I couldn't understand what it was. It came out one day that the very person who was leading the opposition against me didn't believe what I was teaching about the deity of Jesus. I said, 'Well now, just a minute, you're sounding like a Jehovah's Witness.' He said, 'I'd rather read Watchtower literature than what you're teaching us.' And do you know in a strange sort of way it gave me the greatest comfort to know that the one who was leading the opposition against me just wasn't a Christian.

You see this is absolutely fundamental, and you need to know this not least because the Jehovah's Witnesses are still abroad. Once we had them coming up our path and I said to my wife, 'Look who's coming to the door.' She said, 'What are you going to do?' and I said, 'You watch!' They came in and they didn't know I knew who they were.

I said, 'Come in, come in,' and they were surprised as they don't usually get entrées like that!

I said, 'What are you selling?'

'Oh, we're not selling anything, we're here to talk about security.'

I said, 'Well now, let me ask you a question. If I ask you a question and you answer it to my satisfaction you can stay, but if you don't I'll ask you to leave.'

'What's the question?'

'Is Jesus God?'

'Well, it says over here ...'

'Excuse me, the question, is Jesus God?'

'Well, let me just ...'

'Sir, we made a deal, if you answer the question to my satisfaction, you may stay, if you don't I'll ask you to leave. Sir, we made a deal, please leave.'

I don't think he was good for anything for the rest of that day, and that was my purpose! We need to know. John said, 'If there come any unto you, and bring not this doctrine, receive him not into your house, neither bid him God speed' (2 John 10).

How do we come to know Jesus?

Now the way whereby you come to see this truth is when someone points you to this Jesus. The main person to do this in John 1 is none other than John the Baptist. You may be surprised that so much attention is given to John the Baptist in this early chapter of John, but the reason seems to be this. John the Baptist had a great following, and so loyal were some of his followers that they could not bear the thought of following anybody but John the Baptist. So convinced were they that he was a man of God that they knew they had to follow him. After Jesus came (in the meantime John the Baptist was beheaded) and Jesus died and was raised from the dead, there were those who were still following John the Baptist.

So this John, son of Zebedee, makes the point in the early verses, 'There was a man sent from God, whose name was John. The same came for a witness, to bear witness of the Light, that all men through him might believe. He was not that Light, but was sent to bear witness of that Light.' For John, son of Zebedee wants to put the record straight and he wants everybody to know what John the Baptist himself said about Jesus, to bring John's followers back to the truth, and to remove any possible confusion. Because the Jews came to him and said, 'Who are you?' and he said, 'I am not the Christ.'

And they said, 'Well who are you? Are you Elijah? Are you that prophet?'

'No! I am the voice of one crying in the wilderness' (Jn 1).

So John points out that this John the Baptist saw the very truths that John son of Zebedee himself is trying to put forward. In fact the genius of John the Baptist can be summarised in four ways:

First, he too saw the pre-existent Son of God. For he says in verse 30, 'This is he of whom I said, After me cometh a man which is preferred before me: because he was before me.' But that's not all. John refers to this Jesus as the Lamb of God. And so we read it, 'The next day John seeth Jesus coming unto him, and saith, Behold the Lamb of God, which taketh away the sin of the world' (v 29). Now this of course is the language of Zion, but as we saw, we need not apologise for the language of Zion. I'm often told, 'Well we live in a new age; people don't know the Bible,' and I say, 'They can learn it.' And all who become a part of the family of God need to know something about their heritage. This is the advantage of church history and of learning what went on before.

So when John the Baptist referred to Jesus as the Lamb of God it was of course a cryptic reference, not only to the Old Testament sacrificial system, but how the death of Jesus was to be regarded. Hundreds of years before, God gave Moses specific instructions to take a lamb, a lamb without spot or blemish, and take the blood from that lamb and sprinkle it on both sides of the door and on its top. God said he would slay all of the firstborn of Egypt and come up to every home, but when he came upon a home where there was the blood of the lamb, he would go over it. 'When I see the blood, I will pass over you' (Exod 12:13). It was the task of Moses to persuade all Israel to take a lamb and take blood. It was unprecedented—they'd never had anything like it before. And no one knew why that blood would make any difference, but what they found was that the next morning, the firstborn all over Egypt in every family was killed one by one. Those who believed the word and sprinkled the blood on either side of the doorpost and over the top, their firstborn were saved. And this was to pre-figure all that Jesus would be and would do, and John the Baptist saw it in advance that the day would come when Jesus of Nazareth, the Word that was made flesh, would on Good Friday be nailed to a cross. They took spikes and nailed them through his hands against a slab of wood, hoisted it up in the air and dropped it into a hole in the ground, while this Jesus of Nazareth began to shed the blood. It came from his hands and from his forehead.

Nobody could have known how valuable that blood was, more precious than gold, more precious than diamonds. That blood that dripped from the hands and the forehead of the Son of God would make the difference between heaven and hell, between life and death. God promised that the destroyer would come through the world, but 'when I see the blood, I will pass over you,' so that all those who transferred the trust that they had in their works and in themselves to what Jesus did for them on the cross might know that they would be saved.

Just before Jesus died he uttered the words, 'It is finished' (Jn 19:30). A translation of the Greek word *tetelestai* which was a colloquial expression in the ancient marketplace that meant 'paid in full'. When Jesus shed his blood our debt was paid.

Lamb of God. Why a lamb? Charles Spurgeon once

said that the gospel cannot be understood apart from
two words; substitution and satisfaction. Jesus was our
substitute because of his perfect righteousness, perfect
life. Satisfaction, because the blood that he shed cried up
to the throne of God and God's justice was satisfied; and
you'll never be saved until you see the need of a
substitute, and know that he who died paid your debt.

But John admitted that he too needed to be shown
this, for he said twice, 'I knew him not.' So the Holy
Spirit revealed Jesus even to John the Baptist, and the
conclusion of the matter was, 'This is the Son of God.'

The fourth thing that I want to say about John the
Baptist is that he turned all of his followers over to Jesus.
Now this is the point that the gospel writer wants to
make. This is part of his purpose in giving this account
of John. You see, John turned all of his followers over to
Jesus. By the way, this is what Spirit-filled leadership
always does. And I don't mean to be unfair, but it is
corrupt, carnal leadership that tries to amass a personal
following. Reading in the papers these days of the
corruption that is going on in the evangelical world in
the United States, at bottom, the problem is not one of
sex, it's one of money. 'The love of money is the root of
all evil' (1 Tim 6:10). Most of these various evangelists
are trying to do one thing, and that is to convince the
people out there who look on their television screens
that this particular evangelist or pastor is the one that
ought to be supported financially.

You see it can happen anywhere. There are those who
are trying to build an empire and to control people. But
Spirit-filled leadership releases the following to follow
Christ. Spirit-filled leadership sets people free. And do
you know the greatest news that John the Baptist
himself could ever hear was that his followers turned to
Jesus. When he heard that one of his followers turned to
Jesus it thrilled him. This is why he came. He said, 'He is
before me, he is preferred before me. Behold the Lamb
of God, which taketh away the sin of the world.'

Leading others to follow Jesus

But that's not all. John the Baptist spawned an evangelistic enterprise that would end up turning the world upside down. For those he pointed to Jesus pointed their own relatives and friends to Jesus as well. And so the first thing that happened was that here was John, and here were two of his disciples, and he sees Jesus. And he looks at his followers and says, 'Behold the Lamb of God' and immediately they just went and followed Jesus. And then they began to go to their friends and their relatives.

This is the basis of New Testament evangelism—and one of the hardest things I myself ever had to learn. Some years ago, I had to decide on the one hand to follow God and risk losing my reputation and my future, my church and all that it meant to me; or keep up the norm. Arthur Blessitt came to Westminster Chapel. He turned us upside down. But I knew that when Arthur left I had to keep up the things which he had begun.

One of those was God's calling to me to be a personal soul-winner. I always thought myself an evangelist. I'd rather preach the gospel than do anything. I love to preach to the lost. When I think there might be some who aren't saved I preach better, and I always thought that that was enough.

Arthur Blessitt prays this prayer: 'Lord, don't let my vision get broader than the next person I meet.' God was saying to me that I had to be a personal soul-winner. We read in verse 42, 'And he brought him to Jesus.' (It's a reference to Andrew leading Peter to the Lord.) The greatest thing you'll ever do is bring a person to Jesus. Have you personally ever led a soul to Christ? I put that question to our deacons a few years ago, and one of our deacons who was in his sixties, knew that he himself had never led a soul to Christ. But five years ago he went out on the streets, with others. In those five years he has personally led dozens and dozens of people to Christ on the streets, and yet until he was nearly sixty he'd never done it.

Do you know it is the greatest feeling in the world to lead a soul to Christ? Maybe you don't know the day or the hour you were saved, but you will never forget the day or the hour you first led a soul to Christ. But those who discover Jesus are always given the same orders; follow me. One after another heard these words of Jesus; follow me. And that's what God is saying to each of us today. That's what Jesus is saying. But when we go with this message not everybody's going to get so excited. They came to Nathaniel, and they were so thrilled they were sure he would say, 'Great, where is he? Let me meet him.' But his response was, 'Can any good thing come out of Nazareth?' (1:46).

Sometimes you are so excited and you're so sure when you go out to witness that others are going to feel the same way, but it may not be like that. A friend of mine who was converted down in Alabama thought his mother was a Christian, and one Sunday night he was converted at church, and he couldn't wait to get home to tell his mother. He came in after church and said,

'Mother, you won't believe what happened to me tonight; I got saved!'

His mother said, 'Your supper's ready!'

He said, 'Mother, you didn't hear me. I was at church tonight and I got saved.'

She said, 'I heard you, your supper's going to get cold, son.'

He said, 'Mother, I got saved tonight.'

She said, 'I heard you son.'

And he realised that his own mother who he thought was a Christian was lost. Later he led her to the Lord.

But you need to know that not all will react in the same way. There are those who are prejudiced. They still are. Witnessing is not easy. But all of us can do what Philip did. He just said to Nathaniel, 'Look, come and see, come and see.' And it is our task to bring them to Jesus and Jesus will do the rest. When Peter came to Jesus, Jesus just told him that his name would be called Cephas, which means a stone. For once we bring them to Jesus he will take over and do the rest and you never know what God will do with that man, woman, boy or girl that you personally bring to Jesus. He may have a plan for that person you lead to Christ that is greater than he has for you. You may be leading the next Charles Spurgeon to Christ, or the next Roger Forster or the next Clive Calver. You never know what may be in the mind of God for that next person that you personally lead to Christ.

How do you think Andrew felt on the Day of Pentecost when the man he had led to Jesus was preaching the sermon? When we are Spirit-filled, just as John the Baptist didn't try to hold his followers to himself, so when we lead someone to Jesus we will want to see God use them to the full.

Why would anybody want to follow Jesus? Because of who he is and because he knows where he's going and because he knows everything about us. He said to Nathaniel, 'Behold an Israelite indeed, in whom is no guile.' Nathaniel asked him how he knew. And Jesus said, 'Before Philip called you when you were under the fig tree I saw you.' And Nathaniel said, 'You are the Son of God, the King of Israel.' And Jesus said, 'I've got greater things for you than this' (See 1:47–50).

God has a work for you to do that nobody else can do. Arthur Blessitt said that years ago he was on his face before God and asked God to give him a work to do that nobody else will do. And God has used Arthur to witness to Heads of State and to tramps in the gutter. God will use you. God loves every man (as Augustine put it) as though there was no one else to love, and God has a plan for you that nobody else can fulfil. Those who follow Jesus will never be sorry.

A man came into my vestry about a month ago and he

was utterly miserable. He had been attending the Chapel for years, but I noticed I hadn't seen him for a year or two. I asked what the problem was. 'Well,' he said, 'I just don't want to tell you. I'll admit I'm on the fence and I'm on the fence looking toward the world.' He was living with his girlfriend with no plans beyond that, just enjoying life. But he came and heard the preaching of the gospel and he was convicted deeply, and I pleaded with him to get on his knees and pray there in the vestry, but he wouldn't do it. But he did come back to church the following week and the week after that, and something happened to him. Then he came into the vestry and there was a shine on his face. He said, 'I got off the fence—on God's side.'

John the Baptist said that he who came after him would baptise with the Holy Spirit and with fire. Years ago I read a book entitled *I Met a Man With a Shining Face*. It's the story of a man who says when he was a young minister he was given the privilege of sitting on the platform with all the bigshots. And this particular young preacher was feeling so proud of himself. The man next to him (he happened to notice) had such a shining face, and he turned to the young minister who was feeling so proud and he said, 'Young man, have you ever been baptised with the Holy Ghost and with fire?' And the young man said, 'My heart fell and I thought to myself, "I don't know, but if it's what has put a shine on your face, I want it."'

Jesus is the baptiser by the Holy Spirit and he comes today and says, 'Follow me.'

Chapter 6

The Test of Commitment

JOHN 6

What we have in John 6 are the hard sayings of Jesus. 'This is an hard saying; who can hear it?' (6:60). The situation is this. At the beginning of John 6 there were five thousand or more who were following him, but when we get to verse 66 we read, 'From that time many of his disciples went back, and walked no more with him.' Now, why is this? Why do we have teachings in this sixth chapter of John which brought a crowd of over five thousand people down to twelve? Why did Jesus teach like this?

It is his way of testing our commitment. So the question facing us in this chapter is: how committed are you in following Jesus? How far are you willing to go in your commitment? I ask: which crowd are you in—the vast crowd of five thousand, or the small minority of twelve? Now there is a way to tell, and that is by your own reaction to the same teachings that they heard.

The setting is that Jesus fed five thousand with five loaves and two fish and there were twelve basketfuls left over after they were fed, and they all began to exclaim, 'This is of a truth that prophet that should come into the world' (6:14). As a consequence they were determined to make him king, so we read in verse 15, 'When Jesus therefore perceived that they would come and take him by force, to make him a king, he departed again into a mountain himself alone.' So, here were five thousand people that wanted to crown Jesus king. They wanted to do it right there on the spot and they were going to do it by force, but Jesus had another idea. He wanted them to know the main reason that he came into the world.

He deliberately put before them hard sayings. You could say he put his worst foot forward to see how earnest they were. In the meantime he got away from the crowds and later they found him. Now what in fact were these hard sayings?

They actually begin at verse 26 and they continue through verse 65—exactly forty verses, and the effect, I remind you, is from that time many of his disciples went back and walked no more with him. Now what did he say in these forty verses? Were there forty hard sayings? Well, you might say, almost. But it's our task to sub-divide these forty verses and as best as I can tell they come under three categories totalling six hard sayings. The second category includes four of these, and so I come now to the first of the hard sayings of Jesus.

Following Jesus for the wrong reasons

Firstly, there was the painful discovery that there can be wrong reasons for following Jesus—look at verse 26, 'Jesus answered them and said, Verily, verily, I say unto you, ye seek me, not because ye saw the miracles, but because ye did eat of the loaves, and were filled.' Why were they wanting to make Jesus king? Was it because he really was the King of the Jews? Why didn't he let them do it—was it because he wasn't the King of the Jews? Well he certainly was the King of the Jews and he was and is our sovereign King, so in an odd sort of way they were right as seeing him as deserving the kingship, but they were nonetheless wrong in their desire to make him King then. Why? Well there were two reasons for this.

The first is, they didn't care about his glory but their own personal advantage. They ought to have seen who it was indeed that had changed the loaves and the fishes into enough to feed over five thousand, but they saw this miracle as but an umbrella of safety for their future security. They got their tummies filled and they saw in Jesus a free meal ticket for the rest of their lives, and no wonder they wanted to make him king, they thought they were onto a good thing.

The second reason that they were wrong in wanting to make him King then is that they had no concept of the sovereignty of God. They wanted to take things right into their own hands. Wouldn't they know, if they had thought it through, that a man like that, who could perform a miracle such as that, would be God-owned; and wouldn't they know that if this man were the promised King and Messiah that God himself who sent him was big enough to reveal this in his way and in his time?

But it's awfully easy for us, when we see something that may work and we think we have an insight to jump ahead and do things our way. I never will forget a few years ago when I met a particular esteemed Christian who was in this country (his name would be fairly well known, certainly in America). He's regarded by *Time* magazine as the evangelical statesman in America as far as theology goes, he is about seventy, and I just spontaneously asked him this question: 'if you had your life to live over what would you do differently?' He paused and about a minute later he said, 'I would remember that only God can turn the water into wine.' And I think that there is a missing note today among many of us, and I don't want to be misunderstood but I've got to say it in today's preoccupation with signs and wonders. The missing note is the biblical teaching of the sovereignty of God.

I don't know if you're a musician, but do you know what it's like to play the piano when one key is just not working? Perhaps the people who hear you wouldn't know, but you're aware of it, one key is missing. And I think what is happening today is there's something going on that everyone is attracted to but there is a missing note. And what worries me are two things—I know there are exceptions and I thank God for them. But these two things are; first, the lack of undeniable proof of so many alleged miracles and healings that are reported, and, secondly, laying the blame on lack of faith when the proof isn't there.

You see when Jesus healed people it was complete and no one was threatened by the need of verification. And what Jesus is wanting to say is that there's only one right reason for following him. He puts it like this in verse 27, 'Labour not for the meat which perisheth, but for that meat which endureth unto everlasting life, which the Son of man shall give you: for him hath God the Father sealed.' Jesus came to this world with eternity in mind. He came to this world to die on a cross and nothing was going to stop that. We need to be reminded that people can be healed and go on to hell and people can see miracles and get their tummies filled and go on to hell. And what matters today is not whether you're going to be healed but whether you're saved. You need to know for sure that if you were to die today you would go to heaven, because you're going to have to stand before God.

This was the heartbeat of our Lord. He could see what was in their eyes—they wanted the miracles—that which would carry them through so they could just follow their king for the rest of their lives. But Jesus would have done them no favour to let them make him King. It's the worst thing he could've done at the time, and God often does us a singular favour in not granting us our request.

There's that verse in the Psalms, 'He gave them their request; but sent leanness into their soul' (Ps 106:15). Some years ago Dr Lloyd-Jones made the most profound statement I ever heard him utter. He looked across the room at me and said, 'The worst thing that can happen to a man is to succeed before he is ready.'

These people weren't ready for what they wanted, and the Lord knew that and it was love that withheld the request and it was love which led him to teach as he did.

By grace alone

We come now to the second hard saying. In this second category there are four hard sayings, and I would call this category: Jesus' radical teaching of grace alone. The first, which is the second of the hard sayings of John 6, is Jesus' teaching of justification by faith alone. This we examined in some detail in Part 1, but the specific question here, echoed down the ages, is: 'What shall we do, that we might work the works of God?' (6:28). Man always asks that question. We do it to avoid being indebted to God. We cannot bear the thought of being indebted to him and not being able to pay him back. We're uncomfortable when anybody does something for us and we feel we want to get even, and so it is with God.

We all want bargaining power. We want to be in the driver's seat and to negotiate a deal with God. Well, Jesus put it like this, in verse 29, 'This is the work of God, that ye believe on him whom he hath sent.' This is the antithesis of all natural religion—man-made religion— 'This is the work of God, that ye believe on him whom he hath sent.' Now in verse 28 when they asked, 'What shall we do?' we find here what it is in man that tries to negotiate with God. You see the basis of all natural religion is this: that man wants to initiate it. The difference between religion and Christianity lies in who initiates what you do.

I don't care what religion you may want to name, whether it's Islam, Jehovah's Witnesses, Buddhism, or Mormonism. It is all an effort to produce righteousness rather than receive it. In verse 28 when they asked what they should do that they might do the works of God it shows the three things that man always wants to do. First, to initiate things. Second, to control things pertaining to God. And third, to replace the super-natural altogether. To initiate things: what shall we do? To control things pertaining to God: that we might work. And to replace the supernatural altogether: that we might work the works of God. And you see they had no concept of God doing something on his own. That way man gets the glory.

In verse 29 we have the basis of Christianity. Three things. First, that which defies a natural explanation: this is the work of God. Secondly, that which takes glory from us: that ye believe on him. And third, that which gives all the glory to Christ: on him whom he hath sent. You see, what the apostle Paul taught us (and he got it from Jesus) is that: 'to him that worketh not, but believeth on him that justifieth the ungodly, his faith is counted for righteousness' (Rom 4:5). There are so many who are trying to get to God by asking, 'What can I do that I can do the work of God?' And the answer comes back, 'That you believe on him.' Oh no, there's got to be more than that, I mean, what can I do? That you believe on him. It's so humbling.

On one occasion when the children of Israel cried out in the wilderness and they murmured, God sent snakes—poisonous snakes which were biting people so they were dying like flies. And God told them to erect a serpent of brass and hold it up. All the people had to do was to look at it, and those who looked lived. Jesus said, 'As Moses lifted up the serpent in the wilderness, even so must the Son of man be lifted up' (Jn 3:14). It was one of Charles Spurgeon's great sayings: 'There's life in a look.' Man-made religion is: what can we do—we want to produce the righteousness. Christianity is: believe on him whom God hath sent. You see that which gives all the glory to him, that's the object of faith—our Lord Jesus. And this is where truth and justice meet, when this Jesus was lifted up on the cross and he satisfied God's justice.

Only by the Spirit

We come now to the third hard saying, and that is, man's natural inability without the Holy Spirit. In verse 44 we read, 'No man can come to me, except the Father which hath sent me draw him: and I will raise him up at the last day.' Now, what was happening there I suppose is that as Jesus continued to talk the crowd began to dwindle away, and he could sense that what he was saying to them wasn't going down very well. In fact he said to them in verse 36, 'I said unto you, That ye also have seen me, and believe not.' Now these were the same ones then who wanted to make him King. And he now accuses them of unbelief and puts to them what is the most painful saying yet, 'No man can come to me, except the Father which hath sent me draw Him.' And this seems to be one of the hardest of all because in verse 65 Jesus repeated it as if to summarise everything in the chapter. He said, 'Therefore said I unto you, that no man can come unto me, except it were given unto him of my Father.' And we read at the very next verse, 'From that time many of his disciples went back, and walked no more with him.' That must have been the point where the crowd began to dwindle.

Now we might ask this question. What does a preacher do when he perceives the people aren't accepting the truth? Well we should let Jesus be our model, and learn this; he wasn't interested in just holding five thousand people. He knew, after all, that they could only be saved by the truth, and he wasn't there (strange as it may seem to us) to amass a personal following. He came to speak the truth, and this is what gives freedom. He knew that it was the only way that they were going to have freedom, so he wasn't trying to get them to follow him, let them make him King and still be in bondage.

Sometimes we know that we're saying things that aren't very popular, whether we are witnessing to a neighbour or a relative. What do we do? Do we compromise so that we won't be so offensive? But they are not going to be saved unless they hear the truth.

Some time ago, someone brought a young lady to Westminster Chapel to hear me preach. When she heard me preach she was so livid that when they sat down after the benediction the friends who brought her almost apologised to her. I had preached on eternal punishment that night, and this young lady, who was a nurse, said she didn't know anybody believed that and she would never come back here again. She was so angry they couldn't even get her to go back for coffee. During that week this couple said to themselves, 'Dr Kendall does go a little bit too far sometimes in preaching eternal punishment,' and they sent me a little note to ask me to go easy as here they were bringing their friends. But do you know that week their nurse friend phoned them and said, 'I think I'll go one more time' and that Sunday night she was gloriously saved.

The only way anybody will be saved is by the truth, so Jesus just keeps on speaking. In verse 37 he says, 'All that the Father giveth me shall come to me: and him that cometh to me I will in no wise cast out.' And so he just stuck with 'no man can come to me except the Father which hath sent me draw him.' Now Jesus is not talking about one's natural ability to do things. There is at the level of common grace the ability to do things, and this is not what Jesus is talking about. He is talking about our ability to approach the Father. That is not within our power, and there are five reasons that we cannot come to the Father in our own strength.

The first is that being born into a Christian home will not make you a Christian. Back in the 1920s Billy Sunday the American evangelist used to say, 'Being born in a Christian home will no more make you a Christian than being born in a stable will make you a cow.'

The second reason this verse is true is that baptism

will not save, and I have sensed an increase of this teaching of baptismal regeneration. It is not right—it is anti-God.

The third thing: your good works will not save you.

The fourth: your own efforts will not bring you closer.

And fifth: you are blind until the Spirit opens your eyes.

This is what Jesus had to say to them and when you are witnessing to your friends and to your loved ones— which you should do with all your strength—remember that only God can save.

The gift of Christ

The fourth hard saying is that God's keeping grace is by the power of Christ. You see when Jesus said, 'All that the Father giveth me shall come to me', he went on to say, 'him that cometh to me I will in no wise cast out' (v 37). That simply means those whom God saves he keeps saved. But you see this went right against the grain for those people listening and it goes right against the grain of the natural man. The same ones who don't want God to get the glory are those who are intimidated by the teaching that if you're saved you're saved for ever. We want to be able to have control. And these people wanted to be able to stay in control. But Jesus said, 'Come to me and you are mine for ever.' You need to know that if you come to Christ and ask for mercy, he will give it to you and he will keep you.

This takes salvation right out of our hands. There is the residual desire in all of us to earn our own way. But here's the way Jesus put it, 'This is the Father's will which hath sent me, that of all which he hath given me I should lose nothing' (6:39). And in saving us, what is the gift Jesus gives us? Verse 40, 'every one which seeth the Son, and believeth on him, may have everlasting life.' This phrase 'eternal life' is used in fact four ways in the New Testament.

First as it is used in 1 John 1:1—'That which was from the beginning, which we have heard, which we have seen with our eyes, which we have looked upon, and our hands have handled, of the Word of life.' Or as it is used in John 17:3 when Jesus prayed, 'This is life eternal, that they might know thee the only true God, and Jesus Christ, whom thou hast sent.' This refers to the quality of knowing God. The first use that I gave refers to the life of Jesus Christ himself. The second use to the quality of knowing God. There's another use as it is put in Luke 18:30, 'Who shall not receive manifold more in this present time, and in the world to come life everlasting.' It's a reference to eternal life once we get in heaven. We know that once we get to heaven it is eternal—it lasts for ever.

But there is a fourth use of this phrase 'everlasting life', and that refers to the durability of our standing with God. As Jesus put it in John 10:28, 'And I give unto them eternal life; and they shall never perish, neither shall any man pluck them out of my hand.' And that is the way Jesus is referring to it here in John 6. To know that we are saved for ever. I don't know how that makes you feel, but it thrills me. I had someone ask me a few weeks ago, 'What if you want to get out of the relationship? Can you get out of it if you want to?' I said, 'I've got to tell you that it's too late, you can't get out.' They said, 'Oh, that's not right, surely if we want to get out we can.' I said, 'It's like with our children. When she was younger, my daughter would sometimes say "I hate you" and I'd know, well, that's the way she feels at the moment but I'd just love her anyway, and eventually she'd say, "Daddy, I'm sorry I said that."'

And so a person can at a time in his life become bitter and shake his fist at God, but isn't it wonderful that 'the wrath of man worketh not the righteousness of God'? And God knows that eventually we'll be sorry. Peter denied the Lord, but Jesus said, 'I've prayed for you,' and Peter came back.

Having your eyes opened

The fifth hard saying refers to the ability to see Christ's deity, and these last four come under the category of Jesus' radical teaching of grace alone. Now I want us to look here at verse 46. Jesus said, 'Not that any man hath seen the Father, save he which is of God, he hath seen the Father.' There are many references to the deity of Jesus scattered in John 6 and indeed throughout the gospel. Jesus never said, 'I am God'. You won't find those very words, and maybe you wish he had and that would have solved a few problems for you! Well, why didn't he just say, 'I am God'? There's a good reason. Because it only comes by the persuasion of the Holy Spirit. There have been a lot of New Testament scholars, particularly in the nineteenth and twentieth centuries, typified by a German theologian New Testament scholar by the name of Rudolph Bultmann, whose ungodly humanism and liberalism crept into seminaries all over the world. Bultmann taught that we don't really have the words of Jesus, but only the theology of the church, and so the gospel writers wrote down what they wanted Jesus to say. We can't really get to what Jesus said, the writers selected what they wanted to say and interpreted what suited the theology of the church.

Well suppose Bultmann's precis is right for the sake of argument. I ask, why didn't these writers make out Jesus to say, 'I am God'? You see Jesus always spoke of his deity in such a way which, when addedup, could only mean deity. But then we need the Holy Spirit to see it for ourselves—and that's when it sets you afire. For example Jesus said, 'Not any man hath seen the Father, save he which is of God, he hath seen the Father' (6:46). Now Jesus doesn't even say here that the Father is God, but we know that the Father is God because he is described as only God can be described. Earlier it was said that no man has seen God at any time, but Jesus makes it clear he has seen the Father.

Moses once said that no man can look upon the face of God and live. Yet here comes Jesus saying that the Son only sees what the Father does. And so nothing is so thrilling as when you discover for yourself this man who is speaking like this is truly the Son of God, God in the flesh, and when you see it for yourself no one can shake you. And this is why Jesus worded it as he did, so that the breakthrough could come and you can discover it for yourself.

It's what happened to a man by the name of Athanasius, who for a while in the fourth century stood alone in maintaining that Jesus is God and that the Word which became flesh was co-eternal and consubstantial with the Father. They came to Athanasius, the black theologian from Africa, and they said to him, 'The world is against you,' and I imagine he flashed those black eyes when he retorted, 'If the world is against Athanasius, then Athanasius is against the world.' This is what this truth will do for you. But it only comes by the revelation of the Holy Spirit, and it is what Jesus wanted these people to see.

Feasting on Jesus

But I come now to the last category which is the sixth of the hard sayings. I can only refer to it as feasting on Jesus. Now it goes back to the fact that the people wanted to make him king because they'd have a free meal ticket—the loaves and the fishes. And in verse 35 Jesus described himself as the Bread of life, 'he that cometh to me shall never hunger; and he that believeth on me shall never thirst.' Now difficult though it may be for us who are Christians, this may have been for them the hardest teaching of all. They said in verse 31, 'Our fathers did eat manna in the desert; as it is written, He gave them bread from heaven.' And incredibly they had just asked, 'What sign shewest thou then, that we may see, and believe thee?' This shows that the miracles of the loaves and the fishes meant nothing to them; but Jesus ignored that one and just said, 'Moses gave you not that bread from heaven; but my Father giveth you the true bread from heaven' (v 32). And so the point Jesus wanted to make is that it is not getting your tummies filled that matters, it is feasting on him. In verse 48 Jesus repeated it, 'I am that bread of life'. Knowing how they would take this, he baited them and they took the bait and asked the question in verse 52, 'How can this man give us his flesh to eat?'

Then came the most painful statement of all in verse 53, 'Except ye eat the flesh of the Son of man, and drink his blood, ye have no life in you.' Jesus deliberately wanted to separate the sheep from the goats, and he sought out those who would accept him even without their understanding all that he said.

You see what Jesus often does is to put things before us, obstacles in our way that we don't understand, while still he says, 'will you follow me?' I don't think the twelve understood that, when he said, 'Except ye eat the flesh of the Son of man and drink his blood ye have no life in you.' And so he turned and asked them if they were going to go away also. And Peter just spoke up, 'Lord, to whom shall we go? thou hast the words of eternal life' (6:68). Now Jesus might have explained what he meant. What we know is this; first of all that eating was believing. The proof of that is in verse 47, where he said, 'He that believeth on me hath everlasting life. I am that bread of life.' Eating was believing.

Secondly it was a cryptic reference to the Lord's Supper which was to be understood by the Spirit and by faith. So it is not likely that any of the twelve understood it any more than the thousands who said, 'I can't take this, I'm leaving. I'm not going to follow this man any more.'

So maybe we don't understand all that Jesus said. There may be teachings of Jesus that we don't understand. There are things that we don't understand in the

Christian life—why God lets some things happen, why he hides his face suddenly and seems to let us down in our hour of need. I know one existentialist theologian said, 'God's got a lot to answer for,' and he felt he was justified in his bitterness before God.

But you see the difference between the Christian and the non-Christian is this: the Christian vindicates God now—the non-Christian will have to vindicate him later because one day God will clear his name. I don't know how he's going to explain why he lets the famine go on in Africa, or why slaughter takes place in Northern Ireland, the Middle East and South Africa. I don't understand it. But if a detective writer like John Le Carré can keep us from knowing until the last page how it all turns out, and when we read it we think, Oh, why didn't I think of that?—how much more will God, on that last day when he clears his name, show everything. But those who trusted him in the meantime will be vindicated for having done so; the rest will weep, wail and gnash their teeth.

Jesus addressed those five thousand and said, 'Here's what you've got to believe,' but he turned to the twelve and said, 'what about you?' And they said, 'we're still with you.' That's why Jesus does it, to test our commitment. And he comes to us today and says, will you embrace the offence of the cross now and just trust me? And when you come to that stage of your commitment you can say with Athanasius, 'if the world is against me I am against the world!' Peter could say, 'Lord, there's nowhere else to go but to you—count me in!' May God grant that all of us come to a stage of commitment where it is no turning back—for ever.

Chapter 7

Outside the Family

JOHN 8:52–59

We are now going to look at how Jesus addresses certain people who are outside the family. You may be surprised how Jesus does this, and there is surely a lesson for us here. It needs to be said that Jesus is facing a hostile and often learned audience who are not seeking the truth. They think they already have it and their motive is to trap Jesus. Why did they want to do that? They either had to discredit him or get rid of him. The latter ended up being their only option because they were unable to catch him out in any way.

Now it all began when certain scribes and Pharisees found a woman taken in the act of adultery. Immediately they quoted the law of Moses, trying to tempt Jesus so that they could accuse him. They said in verse 5, 'In the law Moses said that if a person commits adultery they should be stoned, and so what do you say?' Jesus replied, 'He that is without sin among you, let him first cast a stone at her.' His approach here was to make them face themselves, and the consequence was that one by one they all dropped their stones and walked away. Jesus looked at the woman and asked her where her accusers were. She replied that no one was now accusing her, and Jesus said, 'Neither do I condemn thee; go, and sin no more.' Verses 12 on to the end record that Jesus then faced this hostile, learned but self-righteous crowd, and spoke honestly to them. Some responded, 'many believed on him' (8:30), but those who hadn't been able to trap Jesus through bringing this woman who'd been found in the act of adultery, were not converted. People like this are always the hardest to reach.

Their basic problem was of bondage, of blindness, and self-righteousness, not that they would acknowledge this. For they say in verse 33: 'We be Abraham's seed, and were never in bondage to any man, and you talk to us about being free.' Well now, if you want to find freedom, the first step is to admit to bondage. Many times we don't like to admit this to ourselves, but you'll never come to freedom until you admit the truth, for Jesus said in verse 32, 'ye shall know the truth, and the truth shall make you free.' You have to begin by acknowledging to yourself what you know is true—you don't repress or push it down into your sub-conscious, but admit it—do you want to be free? Are you in bondage? It may be that you're in bondage to a number of things. It may be you're in bondage to traditions, the way you've always done things. Maybe you're inhibited— maybe you're in bondage to law or to rules—maybe you're in bondage to a counter-productive habit, or maybe you're in bondage to people or to the fear of man where you're always bowing to peer pressure. Whatever it is, you'd like to be set free.

'Ye shall know the truth, and the truth shall make you free,' and the way Jesus introduced this section was like this: 'I am the light of the world: he that followeth me shall not walk in darkness, but shall have the light of life.' With that word in verse 12 he introduced this section that is addressed to the self-righteous Jews who would not acknowledge that they needed freedom. The truth is that these people needed to be convicted of sin, and this is what Jesus was trying to get them to see. In verse 34 he said, 'I say unto you whosoever committeth sin is the servant of sin.' But they didn't see themselves as sinners, despite the fact that they were wanting to kill

Jesus, which, after all is the violation of the sixth commandment. You see when people are blinded by self-righteousness they justify anything they do and won't call it sin.

Once I had a man and a woman come into the vestry and seriously tell me that they were praying about whether to commit adultery. They knew that it was wrong for anyone else, but in their own situation they had a case to be made, which, according to them, God understood. But you see this is what sin does, it is always blinding and will enable us to do things that we never dreamed that we would do.

Here were these people, they didn't consider themselves sinners and yet they were going to kill Jesus. As we have seen some had believed Jesus (8:30), and while it doesn't say what kind of faith that was, Jesus does say to them, 'If ye continue in my word, then are ye my disciples indeed.' They must come out of hiding and become utterly committed, for after all, the most miserable people in the world are not unbelievers but those who have believed and yet haven't become utterly committed. The result for people like that is that they are in bondage. The most miserable person in the world is not the non-Christian but the Christian who is not walking in the light. 'Ye shall know the truth and the truth shall make you free.' And yet it was that very statement that infuriated these Jews because that's when they said (in verse 33), 'We be Abraham's seed and were never in bondage to any man: how sayest thou, "Ye shall be made free?"'

What lay behind all of this that is going on here? Now it would seem, as you read right through the eighth chapter of John, that Jesus has largely wasted his time with those listening to him, after all, you get to the end of the chapter and it says, 'took they up stones to cast at him: but Jesus hid himself, and went out of the Temple, going through the midst of them, and so passed by.' But he spent a lot of time with them. Why did Jesus continue dialoguing with these people? Was it because maybe some of them were converted later? Perhaps—but what else is at stake here? Well, a certain kind of judgement was upon them, and that is the key word to understanding John 8, not only because the word 'judge' or 'judgement' is used four times, but also because it's a frequent word in the Gospel of John. For example in John 5:22 Jesus said, 'The Father . . . hath committed all judgment unto the Son.' In verse 27, 'And hath given him authority to execute judgment also, because he is the Son of man.' So in our present chapter, in verse 26, Jesus says, 'I have many things to say and to judge of you: but he that sent me is true; and I speak to the world those things which I have heard of him.' The key word is judgement and what we need to see is that there was a certain kind of judgement that was on these people even as Jesus spoke to them.

This can happen today. It can happen in a nation, it can happen to a generation, it can happen to a church when judgement is on that congregation. The word 'judgement' has no fewer than five uses in the Bible. The five uses are: retributive judgement; gracious judgement; redemptive judgement; natural judgement and silent judgement.

The judgement of Christ

What is retributive judgement? This is when God brings retribution because his word was violated and it is wrath without mixture, for example 'The wages of sin is death' (Rom 6:23)—retributive judgement—it is judgement without mercy.

Gracious judgement. Well that's partly retributive and partly merciful. You know that verse in Revelation 14:10 where it refers to 'the wrath of God . . . without mixture,' whereas gracious judgement is God's wrath mixed with mercy. Jesus said, 'As many as I love, I rebuke and chasten' (Rev 3:19). Now gracious judgement can be retributive even through sending plagues in order to induce repentance. It can be merciful by mere warning. It was that way with Jonah. God said to Jonah, 'Go', and Jonah said, 'No' and God sent the wind, God sent the fish which swallowed up Jonah, and the fish ejected Jonah on dry land. By this time Jonah had repented and said, 'God, give me another chance.' The Lord came to him a second time and said, 'Go' and this time Jonah said, 'Yes', and then he marched into Nineveh with a message: 'In forty days Nineveh shall be overthrown.' But Nineveh repented and God showed gracious judgement on Nineveh although it seemed at first it would be retributive judgement.

What is redemptive judgement? Well that's a mixture of retribution and promise. I referred in the last chapter to that occasion when the children of Israel murmured and God sent snakes which bit the people so they died. But when Moses lifted up a serpent of brass, those who looked lived, so there was redemptive judgement happening here.

What is natural judgement? That is a mixture of retribution and the consequence of sin: you reap what you sow.

But finally, what is silent judgement? Well, it is postponed retribution, but when it comes it is horrible. The thing about silent judgement is that nothing is happening. It is when God appears to do nothing and this is really the scariest judgement of all, and it is perhaps when God is the angriest. The thing about God is, he never loses his temper, and even when he's really angry he may do absolutely nothing. He doesn't send pain, he doesn't reflect his feelings, he doesn't send calamity. He doesn't even send gracious warning. It is like when sin and promiscuity prosper, God doesn't do a thing. The Psalmist cried out, 'Fret not thyself because of evil men who prosper in their way, for they shall soon be cut down'—soon—ah, but that soon can seem to some of us like an eternity (See Ps 37:7–9).

Twenty years ago one minister in the United States said that if God doesn't judge America, he should raise up Sodom and Gomorrah and apologise to it, for it would seem that sin goes on and on unabated and God does nothing.

The consequences of judgement

Well now, these judgements that I have referred to have their subsidiary parallel and permanent consequences. Part of the fallout from the sin of Adam and Eve was the pain of child-bearing, and man working the cursed ground by the sweat of his brow. Later on God was unhappy with Cain's offering but he gave Cain a second chance, so that this was gracious judgement. But Cain stuck to his guns, and retributive judgement followed and Cain said, 'My punishment is greater than I can bear' (Gen 4:13). God saw man's thought in Noah's day, that it was continually evil, and God said, 'My Spirit shall not always strive with man' (Gen 6:3), and retributive judgement followed. The world was destroyed by the flood, but there was redemptive mercy for Noah's family.

You might be interested to know that the first time the word plague is used is in Genesis 13:17 when Abraham lied about Sarah and referred to her as his sister. When she was taken into Pharaoh's house, God sent plagues, and then when it was discovered who she was the plagues were stopped. It turned out to be that they were a sign of gracious judgement, and mercy was shown to a people outside the sphere of God's covenant people.

The first time the verb 'judge' is used in the Bible is in Genesis 15:14 when God promised to judge Egypt after the children of Israel had been in bondage there for four hundred years. God sent plagues upon Egypt—the first nine of these plagues were mainly gracious judgements—they were warnings. But the tenth plague, the killing of the firstborn, was wrath without mixture. It was retributive judgement, as was the destruction of Pharaoh's army in the Red Sea.

The first time the noun 'judgement' is used in the Bible is in Genesis 18:19 when God showed Abraham what he would do to Sodom and Gomorrah. Sodom and Gomorrah were to go up in flames. There is no sign that Sodom and Gomorrah were ever warned; this was silent judgement, followed suddenly by retributive judgement.

Now one other development that will bear looking into, and that is when God turned his judgement inwardly upon his own covenant people. He said, 'I sware in my wrath that they should not enter in my rest.' This was both retributive and redemptive. But later on came the rebellion of Korah (Num 16) when there was retributive judgement on Korah and his followers and eventually fourteen thousand were killed by the plague. But this retributive judgement became gracious judgement to the survivors, and so at the bottom it was gracious judgement. So you can see that more than one kind of judgement can be in operation at the same time. In Numbers 25 God sent a plague upon Israel for heterosexual promiscuity and idolatry and twenty-four thousand were killed before the plague was stopped; but the survivors repented and it turned out to be gracious judgement.

Now this pattern of gracious judgement, which I remind you is a mixture of retribution and mercy, but always with a warning, is seen right through the period of the kings and the prophets to the prophet Malachi, usually showing itself in bringing about repentance to Israel and sometimes retribution upon Israel's enemies.

People come to me often and ask what I believe about the present phenomenon of AIDS and where it fits into these categories. Perhaps I could just take a few lines to make an application, before we return to John 8. In the present generation I think the lines are not so easily drawn as, for example, between the covenant people of God and those outside this realm. It therefore won't do for us to claim that any one nation can be regarded as being under a special covenant like Israel was. Or to say that God is angrier with San Francisco or Africa or Haiti. Now in order to give an analysis, the question's got to be asked, why all of this now? Why this AIDS phenomenon now? Why not a thousand years ago? Why not a hundred years ago? Why not fifty years ago? According to Romans 1 sexual promiscuity is nothing new, and homosexual promiscuity is nothing new, so why all of a sudden? Well the first evidence of the AIDS virus was in 1979, but the virus may have been present in the 1960s. The same decade saw the emergence of so-called situation ethics, where morals began to break down and the rationale behind it said, 'It's all right in some cases to do this or that.' Of course once that happens the floodgates are opened and the world is never the same again. Right was decided by, 'whatever turns you on'. And I can only wonder if perhaps God looked down on the world he made in the 1960s, when they were saying, 'Make love not war,' and began to send judgement. Who would've thought that they would be saying in the 1980s that it's safer to make war not love.

But what I believe to be true is that the AIDS phenomenon is God's gracious judgement. I would argue that AIDS is the bitter token of gracious judgement rather than retributive judgement, because the AIDS epidemic can be a merciful warning, collectively and individually. Collectively it could signal an end to the permissive age, both for homosexual and heterosexual promiscuity. It may change the lifestyle of millions, and if that happens it can only be seen as a warning—a kind warning—from God. What about those individuals who are (if I may put it this way) unlucky enough to get AIDS? It is not that God singles them out and says, 'I'm going to give you my retributive judgement,' but it could be a gracious warning even to them because they know they've only got a year or so to live, and maybe they'll turn to God, which

many would not do when they thought they had a
lifetime.

So what kind of judgement is being described in John
8? It is silent judgement. Notice verse 15 where Jesus
said, 'Ye judge after the flesh; I judge no man.' Why did
Jesus put it like that? Because Jesus never pronounced
judgement upon one individual except for the implicit
threat of eternal damnation if they didn't believe the
promise; 'For God so loved the world, that he gave his
only begotten Son, that whosoever believeth in him
should not perish, but have eternal life' (Jn 3:16). So
Jesus never singled out another person and said, 'you
are going to hell,' or 'you are being judged.' However,
Jesus never hesitated to pronounce judgement collectively—on a nation—on a city—on a religious group—or
on a generation. This is exactly what is at stake here.

Jesus said, 'I have many things to say and to judge of
you: but he that sent me is true; and I speak to the
world those things which I have heard of him' (6:26). So
Jesus doesn't say what is going on, and there is so much
that he might have said to these Pharisees. But he
opened up the dialogue with the verse, 'I am the light of
the world: he that followeth me shall not walk in
darkness, but shall have the light of life.' Here he put
before them the promise of freedom, but they rejected
the offer. This kind of thing continues right through the
chapter, again and again. No matter what Jesus says, the
Pharisees reject it and want to argue and argue. What
Jesus pronounced was silent judgement, and here's the
way it is put in verse 28, 'Then said Jesus unto them,
When ye have lifted up the Son of man, then shall ye
know that I am he, and that I do nothing of myself; but
as my Father hath taught me, I speak these things.' So
he told them that a day would come when they would
see things as they really were. Now there's no reference
here that the outcome of the crucifixion would result in
all of them repenting, but as Calvin put it, 'Christ simply
put before them the time will come, namely at the

judgement seat of Christ when they would see with their eyes what they ought to have accepted with their ears.' But in the meantime there was nothing. No pain, no calamity, nothing. John said there's coming a day, 'Behold, he cometh with clouds; and every eye shall see him, and they also which pierced him: and all kindreds of the earth shall wail because of him' (Rev 1:7).

Did you ever hear the sound of a wail? You may have heard somebody cry, or someone weep brokenheartedly, but did you ever hear a wail? It's the sound of pathos that will haunt you for ever. Sometimes you hear it when someone is in a car accident and they can't get out, or they're in the flames. I remember years ago, I was twelve or thirteen years of age at the time, I came home from school and saw on the headlines of the local paper which I delivered every day as a paper boy, that my friend Chuck Dickinson had been killed in the Korean War. Chuck Dickinson had been the star baseball player for our baseball team, and he was a household name there in our little town. As soon as I got back from giving out the papers my parents said that we must go and see Mrs Dickinson. Chuck had never become a Christian. Mrs Dickinson had prayed for him for years to be converted and we knew that she would be brokenhearted, so we went to her house to see her, and give her comfort. I remember when we got there we couldn't park within a block of the house, because so many other people had the same idea. So we were a block away, but as soon as we got out of the car, we could hear the most pathetic moan. It went on and on as we got closer. Mrs Dickinson feared that her son would be eternally lost because he had rejected the gospel.

We tried to get next to her when we got into the house and she never knew we were there. The sound of a wail. You see when God exercises silent judgement people just carry on, they laugh, they argue, they enjoy themselves, God doesn't lose his temper. He can wait because there's coming a day, he cometh with clouds, every eye shall see him, they also which pierced him. So what is going on here is silent judgement. Postponed retribution. In the meantime, there is no pain, no evidence of God's wrath. But you can get just a hint of it when Jesus came and looked over Jerusalem and said, 'O Jerusalem, Jerusalem, thou that killest the prophets, and stonest them which are sent unto thee, how often would I have gathered thy children together, even as a hen gathereth her chickens under her wings, and ye would not. Behold, your house is left unto you desolate' (Mt 23:37, 38). Why? Because, as Luke's gospel put it, 'thou knewest not the time of thy visitation' (Lk 20:44). But the retribution came forty years later. So this is what is going on. We must remember that that is always an option when we're talking to those who don't respond, and sometimes we ask, 'Why, God, do you let this happen? Why is it that so-and-so can act that way and there's no judgement, and I do something and God won't let me get away with it for one day?' Ah, 'For whom the Lord loveth he chasteneth, and scourgeth every son whom he receiveth' (Heb 12:6). Those in the family know his chastening as we will see in the next chapter. But you see here are those outside the family. As in Romans 1—God just gave them up.

The children of Abraham

There's one more thing that will bear looking into in John 8 and that is what Jesus refers to as doing what Abraham did. In verse 39 when they said, 'Abraham is our father,' Jesus said to them, 'Well, if Abraham were your father you would do what Abraham did, you would do the works of Abraham.' Now you see, here was the problem. These people thought that they were Abraham's seed simply because they were Jews. They didn't grasp the teaching of Jesus, that the true seed of Abraham came not by procreation but by regeneration. Even so, what makes the person a Christian is not that

he's born in a Christian home, but that he is himself
converted. What makes a person a child of Abraham
(according to Jesus) is not that he's a Jew but that he's a
child of the heavenly Father. Indeed, Jesus told them
that the devil was their father, not Abraham: 'Ye are of
your father, the devil, and the lusts of your father ye will
do. He was a murderer from the beginning, and abode
not in the truth, because there is no truth in him. When
he speaketh a lie, he speaketh of his own: for he is a liar,
and the father of it. And because I tell you the truth, ye
believe me not' (8:44).

But the question I put to you now is this: Are we the
children of Abraham? If we are, there are two things
that we should expect to experience, that is what
Hebrews 6 describes as two immutable things: the
promise and the oath. I want to show the difference
between the promise and the oath, because according to
Hebrews 6 these are two immutable things. Abraham
experienced both of them, and if we are children of
Abraham we ought to experience both.

Firstly, what is the promise? In Genesis 15 we read
that on a clear night Abraham walked out, he looked at
the sky, and God came to him and said, 'Count the stars,'
and when Abraham lost count God said, 'So shall your
seed be.' Now Abraham might have argued back with
God—before I believe the promise, Lord, give me some
evidence—but God said he wanted him to believe his
word. Well, Abraham believed. He didn't have the
evidence, he just believed it. Faith is the substance of
things hoped for, the evidence of things not seen.
Abraham believed.

As we saw in Chapter 2, it counted for righteousness,
and we explored how that became the basis for Paul's doctrine of justification by faith. But what is often overlooked
is that Abraham himself began to have his doubts. Even
after he believed he began to wonder if he had got
it right, and he would say, 'Lord show me one more
time.' Between Genesis 15 and Genesis 22, do you know

God repeated the same promise about ten times? Do you
know what it is like when you get a bit discouraged and
you say, 'Lord, do you really love me?'? And you just
look for encouragement and God gives you encouragement, and you think, praise the Lord! Or maybe you've
come to church and you're wanting to hear God's voice
and you say, 'Lord, speak to me today, I just want to
hear you say that you love me,' and God does.

Well now, this would happen to Abraham. He would
get discouraged and God would come to him and the
promise would be just about like the first one; God
promised to bless him and multiply his seed. But you see
there came a day when God did something else. The
thing about the promise and the reassurance is that they
don't last for ever, by which I mean, eventually you get
discouraged again, and you say, 'Lord, I just need to
have you say it again.' Maybe God has witnessed to you,
or you thought he did, that he was going to do this or
that in your life, and after a few months nothing
happened and you say, 'Lord, would you just show me
one more time?' And he does and you feel good, but
then a month or two later we say, 'Lord was that really
you saying that to me?' Now Abraham was going
through that, and each reassurance helped, but it didn't
last. But there came a day when God swore an oath to
Abraham, after Abraham tried to sacrifice Isaac, and
we're told that when Abraham really planned to come
down on Isaac's back with the sword, God stopped his
hand and said, 'hold it, now I know you fear me.' Then
God came to him and said, in verse 16 of Genesis 22, 'By
myself have I sworn, saith the Lord, because thou hast
done this thing, and hast not withheld thy son, thine
only son: That in blessing I will bless thee, and in
multiplying I will multiply thy seed as the stars of the
heaven, and as the sand which is upon the seashore.'

Now at first glance when you read it you say, 'well, it
looks to me like another promise' but there was a crucial
difference. It was the first time where God said, 'I

swear.' Now this is unusual for God to do. When God swears, he means it, because as Hebrews 6 put it, 'because he could swear by no greater, he sware by himself.' And why God does it is a marvellous thing. He can swear in his wrath and when that happens it is irrevocable, but when he swears in his mercy it is not only irrevocable but the impact on the one to whom he swears is so profound that that person is never the same again. So what is the difference between receiving the promise and receiving the oath? The promise, when believed, does give a measure of assurance, but when God swears with an oath it is full assurance. The promise when restated is like when you hear preaching and it gives reassurance but you need to hear it again, but when God swears with an oath it settles it once for all.

Because we are children of Abraham, we have this included in the promise to us, that God might reveal himself in such an intimate way that all doubts are removed. God can swear an oath to you. It can be at various levels, and it can refer either to your own personal salvation or to what God wants to do with your life, but God can speak in this intimate way, just as he did to me that day when I was driving along and he made known to me just how much he cared for me (see Chapter 3 above).

After that, never again did I doubt his promise. That's what happened to Abraham. This kind of experience results in Jesus becoming so real that you know that he's there; and that's the reason Jesus could say 'Abraham saw my day and was glad' (see Jn 8:56). Jesus was real to Abraham, and so Jesus could say, 'Before Abraham was I am.' Christ pronounces judgement on all who don't believe, and though they may not feel anything at the time, their day is coming. But to those who do believe and walk in the light and know the truth, there's freedom and peace; and Jesus is real.

Chapter 8

Power to Face the World

JOHN 15

In this section from John's Gospel Jesus addresses those in the family and only those. Here Jesus promises power. Do you want power? I think we all do.

Many years ago when John F Kennedy was running for President of the United States, a reporter asked him, 'Why do you want to be President?' And he replied, 'Because that's where the power is.' Jesus promises power, not to those who are elected to political office, nor to those who have influence in the church, but to you and to me. Not political power, not ecclesiastical power. But what kind of power?

Power over people—no. Power in witnessing—well certainly this. But we're speaking of internal power—power within. Not only power to live the Christian life but power to stand above yourself, to have objectivity regarding yourself, to know yourself and to know the will of God and power to face the real world with courage and self-control. Do you want this kind of power? For this is the power that Jesus promises in John 15. And he not only promises it but shows us how to have it.

Power through chastening

Now there are five things that I want us to see in this passage. First, power through chastening. We could say through pruning. In the early verses Jesus said, 'I am the true vine, and my Father is the husbandman. Every branch in me that beareth not fruit he taketh away: and every branch that beareth fruit, he purgeth it, that it may bring forth more fruit.' Chastening—it is the exclusive right of the Christian. 'Now ye are clean through the word which I have spoken unto you.' It is that which the Christian alone experiences. What is chastening? It is punishment for the purpose of correction. Not retributive judgement as I spoke of in the last chapter, where God is getting even, but simply God correcting us because he's not finished with us. It may not bear any direct relevance to anything that has gone on in the past, for though there is so much that we may think God is getting at us for, he doesn't necessarily need a reason.

In the summer of 1956 I underwent my first trial after the encounter with God that I referred to in Chapter 3. That happened in October 1955, but by the following summer things had changed. I had come from Nashville, Tennessee to my home in Ashland, Kentucky and explained to my father the things that God had shown me in his word and he wasn't all too happy about it! What I didn't tell you is that I had been pastor of a church in Tennessee while a student at college. I was the first minister in the family and they had all hoped that I would be a preacher, so when God did call me to preach, they were so proud of me. My grandmother literally gave me a brand new car. I was so proud of that car as I was the only person I knew in those days who owned a car. But the following summer when it was apparent that I wasn't going to stay in the denomination which I was brought up in, as I had seen things which I wasn't happy about, my grandmother took my car away and wrote me right out of her will! Somebody who had witnessed her will told me that when she died, I was going to inherit all her considerable wealth; but when she did die I got one hundred dollars. That was her way of letting me know that she didn't approve of my actions, and she was a godly woman. That summer of 1956 I fell across my bed and I cried out, 'Oh God, why?' I wasn't prepared for anything like this. God had shown me so much and yet my family had deserted me. This has not happened to me just once but two or three times in my life, but at that time I just felt the Spirit say, 'Turn to Hebrews 12:6' (I didn't know what it said): 'For whom the Lord loveth he chasteneth, and scourgeth every son whom he receiveth.'

You see when God chastens you, it's proof you're really his child. There's a verse in Lamentations 3:39: 'Wherefore doth a living man complain, a man for the punishment of his sins?' Don't complain if you're alive and God is dealing with you, it's better than being sent to hell. But this chastening is not retributive judgement, for the psalmist said, 'He hath not dealt with us after our sins; nor rewarded us according to our iniquities' (103:10). Never think that if God lays you low, it's automatically because of something you've done. God's chastening is not his getting even with us. Truth and justice met at the cross. 'As far as the east is from the west so far are our transgressions removed from us' (103:12). It is called chastening, not unlike gracious judgement, for Paul said, 'But when we are judged, we are chastened of the Lord, that we should not be condemned with the world' (1 Cor 11:32). But this chastening can be painful, for when every branch that beareth fruit is purged that it may bring forth more fruit it is a painful process, so says Hebrews 12:11, 'No chastening for the present seemeth to be joyous, but grievous.'

But what is the fruit that God wants? It's the fruit of obedience and it's the fruit of the Spirit, but the fruit of the Spirit should be seen in our making an impact on the world through witnessing and changing the world.

If we do not bear fruit, we are chastened the most severely: 'If a man abide not in me, he is cast forth as a branch, and is withered; and men gather them, and cast them into the fire, and they are burned.' This in John

15:6 is not a reference to eternal punishment, and it is not a reference to purgatory. It is referring to what Paul has to say in 1 Corinthians 3. Picture before you a metal tray with hay, wood, stubble, gold, silver and precious stones on it. Suppose we just mix them all up in this metal tray, pour paraffin on them and strike a match. Five minutes later, what would be left? It would be gold, silver and precious stones. This is what Paul says in 1 Corinthians 3: 'For other foundation can no man lay than that is laid, which is Jesus Christ. Now if any man build upon this foundation gold, silver, precious stones, wood, hay, stubble; Every man's work shall be made manifest: for the day shall declare it, because it shall be revealed by fire; and the fire shall try every man's work of what sort it is.'

This is the terminal chastening we looked at earlier (Chapter 4). I don't know what the fire means and I don't know how it will be manifested, but it will mean that some will be saved, even though they will suffer loss. So Jesus promises power through chastening.

Power through prayer

Secondly he promises power through prayer. In verse 7 he says, 'If ye abide in me, and my words abide in you, ye shall ask what ye will, and it shall be done unto you.' Now this is a verse which has got to be understood in the light of 1 John 5:14–15. You should know that 1 John is really a commentary on the gospel of John, and in 1 John 5:14 we read, 'This is the confidence that we have in him, that, if we ask any thing according to his will, he heareth us; And if we know that he hear us, whatsoever we ask, we know that we have the petitions that we desired of him.' Now both John 15:7 and 1 John 5:14–15 have the word 'if'. It's a big 'if'. Jesus said 'If . . . my words abide in you' and John says, 'If we know that he hear us', we know that what we have asked we will have. Well now, that's a big 'if', knowing that he hears us. It's a big 'if', knowing that his word abides in us. Now not all of us know when we are praying in God's will. Yet I can say this, it is no disgrace not to know. The great apostle Paul (whose godliness I don't think we would question) said in Romans 8:26 'We know not what to pray for as we ought, but the Spirit helps our weaknesses and the Spirit makes intercession according to the will of God.' You see the Spirit is always praying for us, the Spirit is always interceding and he knows exactly what to say to the Father. This is going on all the time when the Spirit is interceding with the Father, and we think, 'Oh Lord, let me know what the Spirit is saying, then I would pray that prayer.'

Both Jesus and John pose the wonderful possibility of doing just that—praying in the will of God and knowing it. It should be pointed out that any prayer prayed in the will of God will be answered. For what we know is that if we ask anything according to his will, he heareth us. It doesn't say we need to know that we're praying according to his will, if we just ask according to his will. We don't always know, but when we do—and there is that possibility —then it is like receiving the oath, as we saw in the last chapter. It is something that can happen in prayer.

And so, you can know that you've got it right even when you are praying. This is the possibility that Jesus puts before us, and that's the meaning of John 15:7 when he says, 'If ye abide in me and my words abide in you, ye shall ask what ye will, and it shall be done unto you.' But then someone says, 'if only I could know if I'm abiding in Christ. If I could just know that.' There is an answer.

Power through walking in love

This brings us to the third dimension of power that Jesus gives us. He promises power through walking in love: 'As the Father hath loved me, so have I loved you; continue ye in my love. If ye keep my commandments, ye shall abide in my love; even as I have kept my Father's commandments, and abide in his love' (15:9–10). And in verse 17, 'These things I command you, that ye love one another.' Now this is the main thing, almost the only thing, to note: to the degree you actually experience walking in love, to that degree alone will you come to know the power of prayer.

Now love is basically three things. First, it is total forgiveness. That's the way the Father loves us. We are forgiven totally, categorically, unconditionally. But we are told to forgive others as we have been forgiven, and this is perhaps the most painful thing in all the world, as I discovered when Josef Ton brought me that difficult but liberating word (see Chapter 3 above).

What does it mean to forgive totally? It means that you refuse to punish. There's that verse 1 John 4:18. Fear has something to do with punishment because whenever you're not made perfect in love, you want to hurt that person, you want to vindicate yourself or show vengeance, either by not speaking to them or exposing them, or even blackmailing them; or saying, 'well, I'll get you for this,' or hoping somebody else does. But what is total forgiveness? God has washed our sins away as far as the east is from the west, and until we learn that and experience it and practise it for ever, we'll know nothing of this abiding in Christ. This is what he means by walking in love.

Secondly, it is refusing to be bitter. Why? Because bitterness always grieves the Holy Spirit. Paul said, 'grieve not the holy Spirit of God, whereby ye are sealed unto the day of redemption' (Eph 4:30). Now it doesn't mean that it separates your relationship with God because we are sealed unto the day of redemption, but we can grieve the Holy Spirit. We have already seen that when we grieve the Spirit we don't know it then; we realise later. Remember we saw that spirituality is closing the time gap between sin and repentance, so that the ungrieved Spirit can work non-stop. And this is what our Lord is after.

But third, love is affirming yourself by being yourself. It is refusing to become what others expect of you, and it is refusing to be motivated by guilt feelings because

another person thinks you ought to be this way or that
way. As Shakespeare put it, 'To thine own self be true.'
You see, when you come to like yourself, God likes that
because he's the One who made you that way. But as
long as you're trying to imitate another person, God
says, 'Oh, you don't like the way I made you, you want to
be like him. But I made him that way, I made you this
way.' It's one of the hardest things in the world to affirm
yourself by being yourself. But God wants us to dignify
his creation of us. And this is love. It is the hardest thing
in the world. It's not trying to be like everybody else.

Sometimes a new Christian will say, 'If I could only
pray like this person.' Sometimes he will pray in a
certain tone of voice trying to imitate another person.
The worst thing in the world is for a preacher to imitate
another preacher that he admires, because you can
never capture the person's genius. You're more likely to
pick up some eccentricity! It reminds me of a powerful
preacher who was out in Texas, in Oklahoma, back in
the 1930s. God was on that man, but he had an eccentric
habit. Nobody knows why he did this, but when he
would get going in his sermon, his left hand would
come up over his ear and he'd just keep on preaching!
Just preaching away! Now that man became Professor of
Preaching at South Western Seminary in Fort Worth,
Texas, and you could always tell one of his students!
Those young fellows were going all over Texas and
Oklahoma and when they thought they were really
ringing the bell, that left hand would come up over the
ear!

Dr Lloyd-Jones told me that back in the twenties in
Wales there was a very powerful preacher, but he too
had an eccentric habit. As he would preach, hair would
get down on his face and he wouldn't use his hand to
push it back, he would just shake it back and so every
minute or two as he preached he would just shake his
head. And he said there were young preachers all over
Wales and as they preached they would shake their

heads! There was even one who was bald-headed, and
he too would shake his head!

Power through persecution

Love is trusting God not to have misfired in the way that
he's made you. But Jesus promises power also through
persecution. He says in verse 18, 'If the world hate you,
ye know that it hated me before it hated you.' And in
verse 20 he says, 'Remember the word that I said unto
you, The servant is not greater than his lord. If they
have persecuted me, they will also persecute you; if they
have kept my saying, they will keep yours also.' Power
through persecution. This is where the water hits the
wheel. We all want power, but must it come this way?
Yes—sooner or later. And I've got to say it, if you're
walking in the light, it is only a matter of time until you
experience persecution—and you may be surprised as to
the origin of that persecution. Who would have thought
my godly grandmother would take that car from me
only because I was trying to follow God?

You cannot avoid persecution. But then if it comes
and you back off and you don't walk in the light, then as
it is put in Hebrews 10:38, 'If any man draw back, my
soul will have no pleasure in him.' Speaking personally,
I can tell you that I never really began to grow very
deeply, so as to know the impulse of the Spirit, until I
faced persecution and did so with patience and love.
Now I know what it is to face persecution, but I can
recall the days when I used to argue back, I'm ashamed
to say. I'd argue back with my dad. I'd say, 'God's with
me and you're doing this to me,' and I'd get mad and
angry, and he'd say, 'Well, it doesn't look to me like
God's with you.' I was being persecuted but I wasn't
facing it with patience and love.

God had been working on me over the years but it
wasn't until several years ago when I began to know a
level of persecution that I thought to myself, 'God's

given me one more chance and God's helping me this time. I'm going to dignify this trial with patience and with love.'

But do you know, the trial actually came in stages. The first stage was when some of my brethren in the ministry began to distance themselves from me, and I was so alone. Then some of my congregation began to distance themselves from me, and that began to worry me. But then where it really began to hurt was when some of my greatest supporters began to back off.

One dear member became upset over a hard decision I had to take. Eventually there were others who felt they must take a stand against what I knew was the leadership of the Holy Spirit. These people felt they too were motivated by the Holy Spirit. I believe to this very day they were sincere Christians. Nobody's perfect.

God only knows what Louise and I went through in those days. I can tell you, that was the greatest trial of my life. But there was a verse that became very precious to me in those days: 'If ye be reproached for the name of Christ, happy are ye, for the spirit of glory and of God resteth upon you: on their part he is evil spoken of, but on your part he is glorified' (1 Pet 4:14). So here are three principles that you need to understand with regard to persecution.

The first is: it is not you that they are angry with. Jesus said, 'If the world hate you, ye know that it hated me before it hated you.' But remember: sincere Christians don't always know it is Christ they are fighting. The second, never take persecution personally. Understand that they've got a problem and that if you were in their circumstances you too would react the same way, and that there's never, never, ever a justification for being judgemental or self-righteous when you're being persecuted, when you would behave exactly the same way. And the third, lovely principle is this: God knows how much you can bear and he's never too late, he's never too early, he's always just in time.

What I was just describing there, we had never had

anything like it in our lives and it became the darkest Christmas we'd ever known. During that time those former supporters sent a letter to all of the members of the congregation, and the letter was so brilliantly written that one of my closest friends said, 'Kendall, if I didn't know you, I wouldn't want you to be my minister.' It just looked like it was all over. A church meeting was scheduled and the place was packed. People came whom we hadn't seen in years, even though they were still on the roll. I let somebody else be the moderator and I just stood back. I watched how the opposition manipulated the Chair and how they were stalling for time because they knew if they had another month or two I'd be finished and out on the streets, and then they would have said it was to the glory of God. But I refused to put my hands on the situation. After two hours when they dismissed for twenty minutes I thought for sure that our time was up, and Louise knew it too, humanly speaking. But suddenly while I was sitting waiting I felt the most wonderful presence right there with me. I could almost touch a being in front of me. I know that when we get to heaven and God lets me see a replay, I'll see it was an angel. And a voice just said, quoting Proverbs 3:5, 'Lean not unto thine own understanding, trust in me.' And ten minutes later, when the meeting reconvened, everything turned around—I still don't understand it. A man stood up and said, 'I move that we vote.' They voted, and the overwhelming majority affirmed us in such a manner that we knew God wanted us to continue.

So remember that God knows how much you can bear.

Power through the Spirit

Power that is promised comes through the impulse of the Spirit. Jesus said in verse 26, 'But when the Comforter is come, whom I will send unto you from the Father, even the Spirit of truth, which proceedeth from the Father, he shall testify of me.' I can imagine no higher level of spiritual living than that of living by the impulse of the Spirit. Well, someone will say, if only I could know the impulse of the Spirit then I'll be set. Quite. You'd be right about that. There is no higher level of Christian living than this; knowing and following through the impulse of the Spirit.

But how? Well, you're going to have to work your way through John 15 to get to this. You just can't jump out at John 15:26. You see, God doesn't lead us directly from A to Z but from A to B and B to C. Jesus introduced the Holy Spirit back in John 14:16. He talked just a little bit about him, and then it's as though he changed the subject. Now why do you suppose he waited until the end of chapter 15 before he came back to the subject of the Holy Spirit again? The power that is promised is not something you can have by just snapping your fingers. There is no formula we can devise. I don't mean to be disrespectful, but it doesn't come by walking to the front and having somebody put his hand on you and have you fall backwards when you're slain in the Spirit. The interesting thing is that today when people get slain in the Spirit they fall backwards. But in the Bible they always fell on their faces.

There are no short-cuts. The power that Jesus promised comes through chastening. It comes through prayer. It comes through walking in love. It comes through persecution. And I guarantee it, when you've passed through these four stages, you will know the impulse of the Spirit.

Remember these two things regarding the Holy Spirit. First, he testifies to Jesus. 'The Spirit of truth, which proceedeth from the Father, he shall testify of me.' And secondly, he leads you to do the same thing that Jesus did. 'And ye also shall bear witness, because ye have been with me from the beginning' (vv 26–27). Don't ask for the impulse of the Spirit if you aren't prepared to be a witness.

Then what? 'Go,' says Jesus. Invade Satan's territory. And I promise, you will not only know the Spirit's impulse, but you will more and more become like Jesus.

PART THREE

WHO'S PULLING YOUR STRINGS?

(Life in the Spirit)

Chapter 9

Forgiven and Filled

ACTS 2

Peter's sermon on the day of Pentecost was climaxed by 3,000 people being converted. Something we should all want to think about.

Who was Peter? He was one of the twelve, he had left all to follow Jesus. He was without doubt the most colourful of the twelve—I would call him a man's man. He's the type of person you'd enjoy being with on a holiday, yet it must be said that he was a fallible man. When he was in the flesh he was in the flesh. When he was in the Spirit he was in the Spirit, and yet it seems nobody could get in the flesh like Peter could. You would have thought that if you were on the top of the mount where Jesus was transfigured before Peter, James and John, that there would be such a sense of God's presence and therefore such presence of mind that no one could make a mistake; but Peter did. He said, 'Lord let's build three tabernacles, one for you, one for Moses, one for Elijah' (see Mt 17:4). It was amazing that he could do that, but it shows that one can be in the flesh even in the presence of glory.

We know about that very sad moment when cowardly Peter denied even knowing the Lord. Using language he hadn't used in years and cursing before a servant girl, he claimed he didn't know Jesus. But when Peter was in the Spirit he was in the Spirit. One day Jesus said, 'Peter,

128 THE GOD OF THE BIBLE

who do you say that I am?' and Peter replied 'Thou art the Christ, the Son of the living God.' This was one time when Jesus could say, 'Flesh and blood hath not revealed that unto thee, but my Father which is in heaven' (Mt 16:17).

Peter was in the Spirit on the day of Pentecost. I think the key to what was going on here was the fact that he was a forgiven man. Only fifty days before, he had denied Christ, and now here he stands before thousands of people, we don't know how many, undoubtedly far more were present than the 3,000 that were converted, and preaches with such authority and with such power.

Peter was acutely conscious of having been forgiven. He had said to Jesus he would follow him all the way, and Jesus replied, 'Before the cock crows you will deny me', and Peter said, 'You don't know me Lord, I love you,' and Jesus said 'Oh yes you will'. When there was the crowing of the cockerel Peter realised what he had done and he looked at Jesus, and Jesus was looking at him, and Peter went out and wept bitterly. On the day Jesus was raised from the dead he sent a special message to Peter, and now on the day of Pentecost Peter has no reason for being self-righteous. He was aware of what he had done and I think that it is part of the key to his power: he knew he had no right to be there.

One reason we ministers so often have no power is because we feel so self-righteous. I know what it is to have a week where I thought I was walking in the light and was free of any bitterness or grudge and I thought, 'well this Sunday I am going to have a great day.' I get in the pulpit feeling so good in myself—and fall flat. And I know what it is to walk into the pulpit on a Sunday feeling so unworthy; maybe it was a busy week and I hadn't been able to pray much, or sometimes just before the service something will happen at home, perhaps my wife and I will be in an argument and I'll get upset with her and feel awful for things that I've said; and then I go into the pulpit and I think to myself, 'I've no right to be here, I can't preach today,' only to find that something takes over when I *know* that I've been forgiven.

Peter did not have a trace of self-righteousness in him that day, he was a forgiven man. But Peter also was the filled man, filled with the Spirit and chosen by the Holy Spirit to stand up and preach. Now all of the 120 were equally filled with the Holy Spirit, but I suspect not all could have done what Peter did. It's a mistake to think that if everybody is going to be filled with the Spirit, everybody can do the same thing. We all have our gifts and our personalities and God always wants us to be ourselves. Peter was the one that was chosen, filled with the Spirit, and perhaps the most remarkable thing about the day of Pentecost, other than the fact of 3,000 being converted, was this—for the first time Peter and the other followers of Jesus in the upper room that day got it all together, for the very first time everything clicked.

Crucifixion confusion

Now the truth is, until that day they did not really know who Jesus was. They could say the right words and know something of him being divine as Peter confessed, but it wasn't that clear to any of them; for one thing, Peter couldn't understand why Jesus died on the cross. There is an old spiritual we sing in the south of the States, 'Were You There When They Crucified My Lord?' The truth is, you could have been there and not seen a thing. For had you been there you would not have known by what you saw that God was in Christ reconciling the world to himself. You wouldn't have felt a thing. It was an awful sight, a crucifixion, cruel, horrible, awesome, you would not have known that atonement was taking place. Even after Jesus was raised from the dead the disciples didn't really know why he had died. It wasn't clear to them. Thrilled though they were, the resurrection had not made clear why he died.

In fact, there were mysterious things taking place over

the next forty days. Jesus would show up and talk to the twelve or to the eleven and then he would disappear. Then when they weren't thinking about it, here would come Jesus again and then he would vanish. One senses that the disciples began wondering what was going on. They were glad that he had been raised from the dead but didn't know what was happening and they all had one question on their minds. It was only a matter of time until it was asked and in Acts 1:6 they said to Jesus: 'Wilt thou at this time restore again the kingdom to Israel?' That is what was on their minds; that is what they thought Messiah had come to do. They saw Messiah as being the deliverer who would emancipate Israel from Rome. Even though Jesus had died on the cross and was raised from the dead they still thought this was the reason Jesus had come, and they wanted to know when it was all going to happen. Jesus replied, 'It is not for you to know the times or the seasons, which the Father hath put in his own power. But ye shall receive power, after the Holy Ghost is come upon you: and ye shall be witnesses unto me both in Jerusalem, and in all Judaea, and in Samaria, and unto the uttermost part of the earth.' This language was quite different and did not cohere with their idea of what the Messiah was to be like.

The last thing Jesus said to them was 'Wait, do not leave Jerusalem.' We don't know for sure how many heard him say that. We know from a comment made by the apostle Paul that at one time there were 500 present who saw Jesus raised from the dead, but I don't know how many heard Jesus tell them to wait. All we do know is that 120 were waiting when the Holy Spirit came. If only Jesus had told them that the Spirit was going to come on the tenth day, and that would be the day of Pentecost, or that after forty days he was to be caught up in the clouds and ascend to heaven, to take his place at the right hand of God. No, the last word was 'Wait, don't leave Jerusalem.' But they didn't know whether it would be one day, two days, or a hundred.

Surprise and stigma

I suspect that, the first day all 500 or however many there were went to that place, they began to pray, excited, thinking that in hours something was going to happen. I suspect after a few days the numbers went down and I wouldn't be surprised if on the day of Pentecost there were those who said, 'I'm going to give this day a miss because there are so many people in Jerusalem today for this feast. We haven't seen them since last year and I will send my apologies, I'll come back tomorrow.' But the faithful 120 were still there. We are told that when the day of Pentecost was fully come they were all with one accord in one place and suddenly there came a sound from heaven as of a rushing, mighty wind. Sometimes God works predictively, sometimes God works traditionally, but no one was really prepared for this, for Jesus had never said listen for the wind; he had never said watch for cloven tongues as of fire on each other's heads; he only said, 'Wait.' It's a reminder that whenever the Lord says to us, 'wait,' this is a specific instruction and it means he's up to something and if we don't wait we will be sorry. I'd hate to be one of those who missed it. But those who went as usual suddenly heard the sound of wind. They'd heard wind before, but this wind was different, an amazing sound, getting closer and closer to Jerusalem, and I imagine they began to ask 'Could this be it?' It was coming in the very direction of the upper room, that room that was so filled with memories. They began to notice something unusual.

Fifty days before these men and women had been demoralised. When they saw Jesus Christ on the cross it made no sense. They thought he was the one that would deliver Israel. They had seen him perform miracles, Peter saw him walk on water and Peter walked on water with him, they saw him raise Lazarus from the dead, they saw him feed the 5,000 with the loaves and the fish;

now there he was on the cross, it couldn't be happening. But suddenly everything is changed. 'Suddenly there came a sound from heaven as of a rushing mighty wind and it filled all the house where they were sitting. And there appeared unto them cloven tongues like as of fire, and it sat upon each of them. And they were all filled with the Holy Ghost, and began to speak with other tongues, as the Spirit gave them utterance' (2:2–4); and as they looked at each other they were filled with joy, no greater than which can be conceived, and all they could think was, it's happening, this is real, it is happening and it was worth waiting for.

But what was happening also that they couldn't have realised at the time, was that the Holy Spirit was ensuring that the church would not only be born in revival, but also be born with a stigma. A stigma is a mark, a public disgrace, something none of us wants. We'll do anything to avoid a stigma, any sense of embarrassment or offence. Many of us hope that the Spirit of God will come down upon our country and that there might be a great awakening, and we may hope that there will be such power that there will be no stigma, no offence. We hope there will be sudden vindication and all will see that there is a God in the heavens. But God wants a stigma to accompany his church. So that which was so marvellous was not received by the multitudes in the way that it was received by those filled with the Spirit. The multitudes were all amazed (2:12), and they said, 'what's happening, what does this mean?', while others mocking, said 'These men are full of new wine.'

What a pity that this would be the first reaction to the church born in revival, that they would be regarded as drunk. But it's just a fact God always deposits a stigma with any great work that he does. The angel came to Joseph and said, 'Don't be afraid to take unto you Mary your wife, that which is conceived in her is of the Holy Ghost, she'll bring forth a son, you'll call his name Jesus for he shall save his people from their sin,' and yet you know Joseph and Mary were regarded in Nazareth as having a baby out of wedlock. Everyone knew that they weren't married and that she was with child and had the baby. A stigma. When Jesus chose the twelve disciples he chose men that didn't do anything for the reputation of Jesus himself. A stigma. You know the church works overtime to erase the stigma, the very thing God wants. Look at the cross, what was more shameful than that? Jesus had promised to his followers of three years that if they followed him they would receive a hundredfold in this life and life everlasting to come. They had trusted those words and now here was Jesus on a cross. Someone shouted up to him, 'If thou be the Son of God, come down from the cross' (Mt 27:40). Some thought he might do just that. I doubt not there were some in the crowd who were nudging each other saying, 'Watch, he will come down from the cross, he's not going to die. This is the man who raised Lazarus from the dead, he's playing games with them, he's going to come down from the cross, you watch.' But he didn't. In fact he cried out 'My God, my God, why have you forsaken me?' (Mt 27:46). People began to look at each other saying, 'Something's going wrong here.' Then he cried out, 'It is finished,' bowed his head, and gave up the ghost. The shame of it all. It didn't make sense. And the cross has always been a stigma.

Paul determined when he went to Corinth to know nothing among them save Jesus Christ and him crucified. We may think that we can go forward devoid of stigma, but God is concerned that we keep it, to keep us humble, and to remind us that we are not going to get our joy and satisfaction from people's applause. Jesus said, 'How can you believe and receive honour one from another and seek not the honour that comes from God only?'

So the immediate reaction to the filling of the Spirit was predictable confusion. It almost always is, and as we look at the sermon of Peter and what takes place in these verses from Acts 2:14–41, we can summarise it in three stages—firstly, Peter's *explanation*; secondly, his *exposition*; and then thirdly, the *effect* of the sermon.

Peter's explanation

So here was Peter, fallible man, forgiven man, filled man; filled with the Spirit which enabled him for the first time to understand it all. It wasn't until then that it all fell into place. Why Jesus died, why he was raised from the dead. Full of the Spirit, the penny dropped, presence of mind came, it all made sense. Jesus was God as though he were not man, he was man as though he were not God. And when he was dying on the cross, it was God punishing Jesus for our sins. He took our place, and at long last everything that Jesus had been saying—the parables, the teachings—came together. Peter had authority, but we must say he was filled with the Scriptures, for, having been called upon to give an explanation, he said, 'Ye men of Judaea, and all ye that dwell in Jerusalem, be this known unto you, and hearken to my words: For these are not drunken as you suppose, seeing it is but the third hour of the day. [It's only 9 o'clock in the morning.] But this is that which was spoken by the prophet Joel; And it shall come to pass in the last days, saith God, I will pour out of my Spirit upon all flesh: and your sons and daughters shall prophesy, and your young men shall see visions, and your old men shall dream dreams.' Full of the Scriptures, so in the course of this sermon he quoted from the prophecy of Joel, Psalm 16 and Psalm 110.

Why do you suppose Peter was able to do that? Clearly he knew the Scriptures before that day. Jesus said in John 14 verse 26, 'The Comforter, which is the Holy Ghost, whom the Father will send in my name, he shall teach you all things, and bring all things to your remembrance whatsoever I have said unto you.' When we are filled with the Spirit, the Spirit brings to our remembrance what is already there. Never think that if you get full of the Holy Spirit you can suddenly quote Scripture, you won't be able to do it unless you knew the Scripture first. We all like to think that if we just pray a little more or get filled with the Spirit, God is going to put knowledge into our heads, but this isn't the way it is. The Spirit enables us to remember what is there. There are times when you may feel the drudgery of reading your Bible or going to Bible study or having to memorise Scripture. But when you are filled with the Spirit, it is then that you will call to remembrance what you need.

But that is not all. By being filled with the Spirit the Scriptures now made sense. For Jesus had said in John 16:13, 'When he, the Spirit of truth, is come, he will guide you into all truth.' The only way we can understand the Scriptures is that the Holy Spirit is our guide, and humbling though it may be for us to have to admit, we all need to be guided. We may think it will be our great brain that will cause the Scriptures to unfold by themselves, but that's not the way it is. Let me tell you my favourite story which illustrates this point.

Many years ago I began to hear of bonefishing. There was something about catching a bonefish which had a ring to it because I had been told it was quite an accomplishment. No one should go without a guide, because the fish are very hard to catch and very difficult to see. The idea is that you don't just throw out your line and wait for the fish to pick up the bait, but you look for the fish. It's the only sport that simultaneously combines hunting and fishing. You literally look for the fish in crystal clear water. It's very shallow water, maybe twelve inches deep, and you look for a fish in the water, but they're very skittish and the slightest sound causes them to take off like a torpedo, so you've got to be very quiet. I was fascinated by that so I said I was going to go bonefishing, and my friend who was with me told me I shouldn't go without a guide.

I said, 'Well, I've read a couple of articles in fishing magazines. I think I know what to do.'

'Well,' he said, 'I think you're wrong, you need a guide.'

I went to the fishing camp and I said to the manager, 'I want to go bonefishing.'

He said, 'Who's your guide?'

I said, 'I don't have a guide.'

He said, 'Are you a bonefisherman?'

I said, 'Will be after today.'

He said, 'Have you ever been bonefishing before?'

I said, 'No.'

He said, 'Nobody goes bonefishing without a guide.'

'Look,' I said, 'I'll be all right, will you rent me a boat?'

'Sure I'll rent you a boat,' he said.

I said, 'Will you just tell me where to go?'

So he got a map, he told me where I would find thousands of bonefish.

So I took the boat out all by myself and I began to look. I started out at 8 o'clock in the morning, I came back at 8 o'clock at night, and went to the manager of the fishing camp.

He said 'How many did you catch?'

I said, 'There weren't any.'

He said he thought there were and told me to go and have a look in the ice house. I went and there was a big bonefish that was prepared to be mounted.

I said, 'Where was it caught?'

He said, 'Right where you were, they were all around you.'

I said, 'I didn't even see any.'

'I told you you ought to have a guide,' he said.

That made me so mad I thought I'd never go bone-fishing again. But a week or two later I thought I'd give it one more try, read one more article about what I was doing wrong. Do you know, the same thing happened— I didn't even see them. I'm ashamed to say how many weeks and months I went because I didn't want to pay the price of the guide and I didn't want to admit I had to have a guide. I've always been able to do things myself, thank you. But one day I finally knew I was beat. We hired the best guide in the Florida Keys.

I said, 'Where shall we meet?'

He named the place—same as before.

I said, 'Well there's no use going there, I've been there for six months, there are no fish there.'

He said, 'Just be there.'

I was there. He started up the motor, chugged to the spot where I had been fishing for months, and turned off the motor.

He said, 'Shush, 10 o'clock, sixty feet to the stern of the boat.'

I said, 'Where? I don't see.'

'There he goes, nine pounder, see him?'

'No,' I said.

'It's all right, you'll see another one in a minute,' he said.

Five minutes later.

'Bonefish, 3 o'clock, coming across at 2, 1,' he said.

I still don't see it.

He said, 'All right Kendall, there's a bonefish coming, he's a hundred yards away, he's now at 12 o'clock, you just look at that spot at 2 o'clock. He said 1, 1.30, there!' And I saw a dark shadow go across the spot.

So that's a bonefish! Before the day was over I actually hooked five for myself. What made the difference? I had to have a guide.

Paul says, 'The natural man receiveth not the things of the Spirit of God: for they are foolishness unto him' (1 Cor 2:14), and we may think that because we've read one or two books we are going to understand the Bible. Maybe you are good in architecture. Maybe you are good in history or philosophy, and then when it comes to the Bible you read it and you say it makes no sense. But when the Spirit is come you'll go back to the very same Scriptures which were a mystery to you and suddenly the meaning is unfolded. This is how it was that Peter, who hadn't understood anything until that day, was able to say that what the Bible said would happen is happening now.

Peter's exposition

The church was not only born in revival and born with a stigma, but it was born with expository preaching, and that is what Peter was doing on that day. At the end of the quotation of Joel came this, 'Whosoever shall call upon the name of the Lord shall be saved.' That was the key that led Peter to move in to what Jesus had come to do, to seek and to save that which was lost.

For Peter—forgiven man, filled man, full of the Spirit, full of the Scriptures—was also full of Jesus. There is the reason for his authority: he was full of Jesus. For now Jesus was as real to him in the Spirit as he had been to Peter in the flesh for the previous three years. When Jesus was saying that the Spirit would come he put it like this, 'A little while and ye shall not see me, and again a little while and ye shall see me, because I go to my Father.' And you know the disciples got into a huddle and they said 'Did you hear that? A little while and we won't see him and a little while and we will. What does he mean?' These disciples were so depressed over everything that Jesus was saying about the Holy Spirit. In fact, Jesus said, 'Sorrow has filled your heart because I'm talking to you like this' (see Jn 16). You couldn't have convinced them then that the Spirit would make Jesus so real to them that they would not even want to bring him back from heaven. But that's the way it was, and so full of Jesus was Peter that it was reflected on his face, so when he quoted Psalm 16 where David said, 'I saw the Lord always before me', Peter understood what that meant. For the whole time Peter was preaching he was looking at Jesus, Jesus was right at his side, and the Lord was so real that Peter had an authority and a fearlessness. Jesus was more real to him than Peter's own existence. And so Peter's message could be summarised by saying two things.

Peter's effect

First, something happened to Jesus and secondly, something happened to Peter. Verse 32, 'This Jesus had God raised up, whereof we all are witnesses.' Something happened to Jesus, something happened to the disciples, and I suspect the audience was more interested in what had happened to them because they were amazed that Peter could talk like this. They were amazed that this man, a fisherman, unlettered, regarded as ignorant by the priests, could speak with such boldness and honesty and with such a shine on his face. You see at that stage they weren't all that interested in what had happened to Jesus, they didn't care anything about him. They didn't like him. They hated him, they didn't want his name mentioned. But they *were* interested in what had happened to Peter. That gripped them. We may think that the world is going to be interested in our Jesus, and we want them to be, but they're not going to be asking questions about him until they see that we are transformed, and that's what fascinated these people now. They were looking at Peter.

I never will forget how Arthur Blessitt had been walking through Aman, Jordan. Tired and thirsty, he put his cross down in front of the Holiday Inn in Aman. The place was being heavily guarded, and he found out later the OPEC ministers' conference was there. Arthur was surprised he got in, he was dirty, wearing jeans and a T-shirt. He was thirsty so he went downstairs to the bar and asked for a coke, and was sitting at the end of the bar drinking his coke when an Arab Sheikh walked over to him and said, 'I want what you've got'. Arthur asked him exactly what it was he meant. The Arab said that Arthur had something he wanted, there was a shine on

Arthur's face. Arthur told him he was a follower of Jesus Christ and began to witness to him. The Arab prayed to receive Christ and it turned out he was an official with the OPEC ministers. For the next three days Arthur spent the whole time ministering to those oil men. They wouldn't have been interested in Jesus until they saw Arthur's face.

So it is here, where the multitude wanted to know how they could have what had happened to Peter. It was at this point Peter said, 'Repent'. Change your mind. You need to change your mind about Jesus of Nazareth, because you took him and crucified him, but God has made that same Jesus, whom you crucified, both Lord and Christ. God allowed Jesus to be pierced and spat upon and hated, but now he has raised him from the dead, now Jesus is at the right hand of God, and God tells us to bow down to him. Repent, be baptised and you will receive the gift of the Holy Spirit. When the multitude heard this, they were cut to the heart. The Bible says that the word of God is quick, powerful, sharper than any two-edged sword, piercing even to the dividing asunder of soul and spirit and of the joints and marrow, and is a discerner of the thoughts and intents of the heart. Jesus said, 'When the Spirit has come it will reprove the world of sin, of righteousness and of judgement.' It's the Spirit that makes a man see that he is lost. It's the Spirit that shows him his sin. It's the Spirit that convicts him of righteousness. It's the Spirit that lets him see there is judgement to come. The Spirit alone will convince people. We can argue until we're blue in the face—'a man convinced against his will is of the same opinion still'—but when the Spirit is there he will be cut to the heart and will say, 'what shall I do?' Nobody was laughing now. Nobody was mocking. They were convicted, concerned ('What shall we do?') and converted— it says they gladly received his word. Then they confessed, and as many as gladly received his word were baptised, right on the spot. (Whoever came up with this idea that you wait months and years to be baptised after you've been converted?) They did it right on the same day.

Who's pulling your strings? The Holy Spirit pulled the strings of Peter's heart; he obeyed the impulse of the Spirit and preached with power. The Spirit began to pull on the strings of hearts who listened, and they realised that this was a very serious matter. What shall we do? Maybe you've seen Christianity as an optional thing and you have mocked and you've laughed. May God grant that the Spirit comes on you to convict and to give you a concern that you cry out 'What must I do?', because there is most surely judgement to come.

Chapter 10

Knowing the God of Glory

ACTS 7

In the Gospel of Matthew Jesus says, 'When they deliver you up, take no thought how or what ye shall speak, for it shall be given you in that same hour what ye shall speak. For it is not ye that speak, but the Spirit of your Father which speaketh in you' (Mt 10:19).

There will be times, then, when we should take no thought but let the Spirit control us. Who's pulling your strings? We know this, that the impulse of the Spirit is available to each of us, and what we are looking at in this section are demonstrations of how one can discern and follow the impulse of the Holy Spirit. This was the case with Peter in the last chapter and so with Stephen now.

Stephen stands before the Sanhedrin; it is his one opportunity to address the same body of men that ordered the crucifixion of Jesus. What an opportunity this was; as far as we know Stephen was the first person ever to have this privilege. He was charged with blasphemy and wanting to destroy the temple and change all the customs which Moses had delivered to them. The High Priest had just one question, and from that moment on Stephen spoke. The question was, 'Are these things so?'

The charge against Stephen

Who was Stephen? He was one of the original seven deacons. The trouble all came about because of the first family quarrel in the church. Some widows were apparently overlooked in the daily distribution of food. No doubt the devil got in; no doubt the devil took advantage of some discontent, and it was his strategy to bring the church into chaos and cause disunity. But the devil always eventually overreaches himself. One thing about the devil, he never learns. One would think he would learn from his past mistakes but he never does, and the result eventually here was the conversion of Saul of Tarsus.

I'm not interested in settling the issue as to whether Stephen was what some of us would call a layman. If you're in the free church tradition you would probably refer to Stephen as a layman. If you're in the Anglican tradition you would have a rather different status for Stephen. What I do know is that the job description for the deacon was waiting on tables. Those too lofty for that need not apply. What I also know was Stephen's willingness to wait on tables. Now as you look at Acts 7 you find here a man who knew his Bible backwards and forwards. Here was a man who was qualified. You could say over-qualified to be a deacon, but he was willing and it was in fact that which led to the greatest opportunity one could possibly imagine. So Stephen's being willing to wait on tables led him to greatness.

I wonder if you feel yourself over-qualified for something that is available to you. Maybe you're needed in a particular moment for a particular job but you feel you are able to do something better than that—it would be a waste of your gift. Well, if you are afraid that your gift will be unnoticed, just remember Jesus said, 'He that humbleth himself shall be exalted, he that exalteth himself shall be abased' (see Mt 23:12). And those who are seeking a high profile in the kingdom of God will sooner or later be abased.

Stephen never dreamed that one day he would be addressing the Sanhedrin, but he soon got into trouble. We read that as soon as the deacons were chosen the word of God increased, the number of the disciples multiplied and Stephen, full of faith and power, did great wonders and miracles among the people. Never think that if the Spirit comes down in great power and we see the unusual, signs and wonders, that this is going to stop all the mouths of our critics. Never think that an undoubted outpouring of the Spirit will cause the whole world suddenly to want to be Christian. This was happening here and the consequence was that they were angry with Stephen. We are told they were not able to resist the wisdom and the Spirit by which he spoke. You may think that if you've the word to be spoken and you've given an answer, it will silence your critics for ever; but here that just made them all the more angry.

Now we come to the accusation. It was put informally in verse 11 of chapter 6, 'We have heard him speak blasphemous words against Moses, and against God.' It was put more formally in verses 13 and 14, and yet by false witnesses who said, 'This man ceaseth not to speak blasphemous words against this holy place, and the law: For we have heard him say that this Jesus of Nazareth shall destroy this place [the temple], and shall change the customs which Moses delivered us.' And so the whole accusation was false. There was nothing really truthful about it. No doubt Stephen had said certain things that suggested that Jesus Christ had fulfilled the Law, and no doubt Stephen had said that our worship is to be in the Spirit and not in a temple, but we are told these were false witnesses. It's a marvellous thing when you are falsely accused, it means that you're in the tradition of our Lord Jesus. Peter said, 'If ye be reproached for the name of Christ, happy are ye; for the spirit of glory and of God resteth upon you: on their part he is evil spoken of, but on your part he is glorified' (1 Pet 4:14).

Stephen's reaction

The best guarantee of God's anointing is that these two things are true:

1 Someone lies about you.
2 You take it gently and refuse to defend yourself.

Stephen had an opportunity to defend himself, but he never did. He might have addressed the very accusation of these men and proved that he was innocent of the charges. He could have won the battle but he would have lost the war. The best guarantee of God's anointing is when they lie about you and you take no notice of that and never try personally to defend yourself but stick to the issue. The secret of Stephen's power and anointing as is seen throughout this chapter is explained in the very last verse when they stoned Stephen and he knelt down and he cried with a loud voice, 'Lord, lay not this sin to their charge.' In this he disclosed the secret of his power. The greatest thing any Christian can experience is that God's ungrieved Spirit may in-dwell him in great measure, when the Holy Spirit is utterly and completely himself in him.

Now we have said before that the Holy Spirit is a very sensitive person. We sometimes look at an individual who is very sensitive as insecure, and we regard it as not a very happy quality if a person is too sensitive. But you need to know that the Holy Spirit is like that. You may not think it is a very attractive quality about him, but that's the way he is. He is very sensitive, and the primary way we grieve the Spirit is by bitterness, when we do not forgive those who have hurt us. The thing about bitterness is that it always seems right at the time. Whenever we are bitter we can't see that God does not condone our bitterness because we're so keenly aware of our feelings. We just imagine God feels the same way, whereas in fact he has just backed off. We realise later that is what happened. But God is no respecter of persons and none of us can bend the rules, for if I am bitter I will grieve the Spirit and not have the anointing upon me.

Maybe you admire Stephen—the secret of his power was that at the end of it all, the last thing he wanted to do was to pray, 'Lord, don't hold against them what they are doing.' He really meant that. When Jesus said, 'pray for those who despitefully use you,' he really meant it. If you say, 'OK Lord, bless them' and then if he does you say, 'Well Lord I didn't really mean you to bless them', that's no good. You see, when you mean it you will be glad when they are blessed. Stephen didn't want these men to be punished, and as long as we are wanting those who have hurt us to be punished we have tied God's hands and he is not free to be himself in us. But God was free to be himself in Stephen, and we are told that as they were bringing the accusations before him, an unusual phenomenon emerged: 'All that sat in the council, looking stedfastly on him, saw his face as it had been the face of an angel' (6:15). I'm not sure that I understand that but I believe it. I only ask, how could men like that proceed with their questions? These men knew their Old Testament, they had to know about Moses when he came down from Mount Sinai and his countenance was glistening, they had to have thought of Moses. How could they go on? You would have thought at that moment that they would be on their knees. But these were not godly men. Jesus said that evil men would grow worse and worse. So the High Priest continued, 'Is it so?'

The God of glory

I want to make some observations on Acts 7. The first is that the chapter begins with a reference to the God of glory and it ends with the reference to the glory of God, verse 55. There is a hint here for us. If we want to see the glory of God we should know something of the God of glory, and I fear that an unhappy difference with so many of us compared to Stephen is that we are experts in speaking of the glory of God but not in seeing it.

What do you suppose was the first thing that crossed Stephen's mind when it came to describing God? Jesus said that out of the abundance of the heart the mouth speaketh. If you had to fill in the blank and come up

with the one word above all of this that best describes the
God of the Bible what word would you use? Well, the
best single word to describe the God of the Bible is glory
and that is what Stephen said, 'Men, brethren and
fathers, hearken; the God of glory appeared unto our
father Abraham' (7:2).

Now there is so much that we could say about this
word. In the Hebrew it comes from a word which means
'heaviness'. When someone is described as being very
weighty, a very heavy figure or a person who throws
their weight around, that is the idea here. But in the
Greek it comes from a root word that means 'opinion',
so if you were simply going to come up with what the
word 'glory' means etymologically you would have to say
it meant 'weighty opinion'. But the glory of God is the
sum total of all his attributes, and I think after all is said
and done, it comes down to two things:

(1) His mind. That is his will, what he wants, what he is
up to. You could say the glory of God is the dignity of
his will.

(2) It's the very way he manifests himself. The way he
chooses to reveal himself.

When we get to know God we discover that the
greatest thing about him is his glory, and we want to see
that glory. Moses one day put before God a stupendous
request, he said in Exodus 33:18: 'I beseech thee, shew
me thy glory.' God said, 'I will make all my goodness
pass before thee, and I will proclaim the name of the
Lord before thee; and will be gracious to whom I will be
gracious, and will show mercy on whom I will show
mercy.' It's God's way of saying to Moses that nobody
has an inherent claim upon him. Never say that God
owes you something. As long as you feel that God owes
you something, you betray the melancholy fact that you
have not seen his glory. God owes us nothing and has a
right to do as he will with any of us. He said, 'I will be
gracious to whom I will be gracious, and will have mercy
on whom I will have mercy.' When you understand that

about God it will bring you to your knees and you will ask him for mercy. Nobody has an inherent claim upon the God of glory.

However, those Stephen was addressing thought they did. The Sanhedrin really thought that if God did anything worthwhile in this world he would do it through them, and that they would be the first to know what God was up to. They thought they had an exclusive franchise on the God of glory, and yet here they were having to listen to a nobody who obviously wasn't afraid of them, knew his Bible better than they did, and started out talking about the God of glory. Stephen began by reminding them that the God of glory appeared to Abraham. I don't know how—it may have been through brilliant brightness. Moses had a glimpse of God's glory and he said, 'When I heard the thunderings of Sinai and saw the lightnings, I did exceedingly fear and quake.' Isaiah had a glimpse of God's glory (Is 6:1–5) when he saw the seraphim with six wings, two with which to fly, two with which to cover their feet and two with which to cover their eyes. They cried one to another 'Holy, holy, holy is the Lord of hosts: the whole earth is full of his glory'; and Isaiah cried out, 'Woe is me! for I am undone,' for that is the inevitable effect when we see the glory of God: we see our unworthiness and our sinfulness. Ezekiel saw the glory of the Lord and he said, 'I fell on my face' (Ezek 1:28). John on the Isle of Patmos saw the glorified Lord and he said, 'When I saw him, I fell at his feet as dead' (Rev 1:17). How did God reveal himself to Abraham? Maybe it was through what became known as the Shekinah glory.

Many years ago in my home church in Kentucky, on 13th April 1956 we had a service that was to change my life. Some men had been in an all night prayer meeting the night before the service, and as people were singing in the middle of the service three or four of these men did something quite unthinkable. They stood up and asked the song leader to stop. One of the men began to exult as he walked back and forth in the aisles. For a

period of maybe ten minutes a haze came down on the
service, like a golden cloud. Those who were at the front
of the church said they could not see all the way to the
back and those at the back could not see all the way to
the front. Such power was present. It was a life-changing
evening for many people.

So far as I know that haze never reappeared, and
while I don't understand it I do know this, that in the
days of the early Methodists this kind of phenomenon
or its equivalent was not uncommon. I know that there
was once a tent meeting in the hills of Tennessee, when
there was such a presence of God on the tent that those
outside could see a glow over the tent while the services
were being held. Time after time people would come to
that tent meeting determined to tear it down, some
would actually go to the ropes and try to tear down the
tent, only to be converted before the evening was over.
They dare not get near that place for they'd get saved.

My own background is the Church of the Nazarene, a
small denomination. But back in the 1920s in America it
was the fastest growing denomination in the United
States. They were seeing more people converted than anybody. Now in the latter days of Phineas Bresee the
founder of that denomination, he would go from one
church to another with one message. It was this, 'Keep the
glory', for he knew that if those early Nazarenes lost that
they were finished. They didn't have any great intellects,
they didn't have any monied people, they were just simple
people of the lowest social economic class, but they had
one thing: 'the glory'. Phineas Bresee knew if they lost
that they were finished and, I would add, so are we. The
question is, will we see the glory of God?

What is Stephen's main point in this long sermon? It's
almost totally quotation of Scripture. As best as I can
figure out, there are two themes. One is the preservation
of God's true people. The other is that those within the
covenant family are not allowed to bend the rules, that
God is no respecter of persons. So we're shown that God
preserves his family and that God judges those outside

the family who persecuted it. As we see in verse 7, God said to Abraham, 'the nation to whom they shall be in bondage will I judge, and after that shall they come forth, and serve me in this place,' a reference to the fact that the children of Israel would be in Egypt for 400 years under Pharaoh's bondage but that God would deliver them and then judge Pharaoh. So the theme is the preservation of God's people and how he will judge those outside the family.

But the second theme of the seventh chapter of Acts, and it's the main one as far as Stephen appears to be concerned, is that God equally judges unrighteousness within the family. For example, in verse 40 there was the occasion when Aaron had listened to the children of Israel when they said 'Make us gods to go before us: for as for this Moses, which brought us out of the land of Egypt, we wot not what is become of him. And they made a calf in those days and offered sacrifice unto the idol, and rejoiced in the works of their own hands. Then God turned, and gave them up to worship the host of heaven.' This is just one example that Stephen cites to show that God will judge any unrighteousness within the family.

So we have here in the seventh chapter of Acts two kinds of traditions. There are those who are actually in the spiritual line of Abraham—Isaac, Jacob, the twelve tribes, and Moses; then there are also those who think they're in that tradition but are, in fact, in opposition to it. What Stephen is showing is that there is a preservation of God's family, his true people, through Abraham, Isaac, Jacob, Moses, and there is a historical line, a continuity of the God of glory at work. But there was always opposition to that. Stephen even cites how the brothers of Joseph betrayed him to demonstrate the theme that there were always those within the family who would oppose what God is up to.

Jonathan Edwards believed that the task of every generation is to discover in which direction the Sovereign Redeemer is moving, then to move in that direction. There were always those who weren't convinced about

what the Sovereign Redeemer was doing, so they would
oppose it and claim to be upholding the historical tradition. Jonathan Edwards said 'When the church is revived
so also is the devil' and whenever God is up to something
and begins to show his glory there will always be opposition to it. And those people who oppose what God is
doing always claim to have antiquity on their side and to
be showing continuity with Abraham, Isaac and Jacob.

So the Sanhedrin said they were the ones that God
used. Stephen had his work cut out for him to show that
whenever God was doing something there was always
opposition to it.

When we get to the present day one must be very
honest and ask, 'Am I really in the tradition of
Abraham, Isaac, Jacob; am I really following the Lord,
or could it be that I am an heir to a tradition of
opposition?' Jesus put it like this: 'Woe unto you, scribes
and Pharisees, hypocrites! because ye build the tombs of
the prophets, and garnish the sepulchres of the righteous, And say, If we had been there in the days of our
fathers, we would not have been partakers with them in
the blood of the prophets' (Mt 23:30–31). In other
words, 'If I had been there I wouldn't have been on the
side of those who persecuted the prophets, I would have
been on the side of the prophets.'

You have this all the time. Some people will extol a
great man and claim him a hero, for example there are
those who admire Whitefield today and want to be in his
tradition, but there is reason to believe that they would
have been among those who were opposing Whitefield
had they been alive at the time.

This is what Stephen was having to fight against. He
knew that he was in the biblical tradition and he knew
that Jesus Christ was the Son of God and that Jesus had
fulfilled everything the Old Testament prophets had
forecast. And he knew that those he was addressing
were opposed to that very tradition, although they
thought they were upholding it.

I sometimes wonder how the question can be

resolved, 'who is God with?', when you have those who are opposing you and yet they are saying all the right things and quoting the right Scriptures. At the end of the day the only way to begin to believe that God may be with us is that we are like Stephen who could say, 'Lord, lay not this to their charge', for as long as you are on at God to punish those who oppose you, you are no different from them. Well, perhaps Stephen wasn't very subtle when he put himself clearly in the tradition of Abraham, Isaac, Jacob, Moses and made it very clear where the Sanhedrin stood. Stephen might have played it differently—as I said, he might have won the battle. These religious people could take it no longer. We are told in verse 54 that when they heard these things they were cut to the heart. One wishes that when anyone is cut to the heart it would always mean that they'll be converted, but obviously that is not true. The Authorised Version says, 'they gnashed on him with their teeth', the translation possibly is 'they gnashed at him', they gritted their teeth at him, they were so angry. The Sanhedrin didn't think much of Stephen's sermon but you can get a good idea of what God thought of it, for at this moment something happened to Stephen. He began to look up and saw the heavens open. He said 'I see the Son of man standing on the right hand of God,' and that was all they could take, they stopped their ears and screamed in a frenzy. But what a sight it must have been for Stephen; the stigma was worth it all.

Why was Jesus standing? We can't be sure—perhaps he stood because suddenly he wanted to show the interest he had in Stephen. We all know what it is to be in a large crowd and if some commotion takes place at the other end, people will stand, and it could be that this was symbolic of how our Lord feels—when he sees us suffer he stands. Or the better explanation of his standing may be simply that Jesus was standing to get ready to welcome home the first martyr. What a sight it was that this man who could begin talking about the God of glory would in the end see the glory of God. He fell asleep. He lost his life over it. He lost the battle but he won the war.

Chapter 11

Obedience and Opportunity

ACTS 17

'And they that conducted Paul brought him unto Athens: and receiving a commandment unto Silas and Timotheus for to come to him with all speed, they departed' (17:15). Paul was alone. He had time on his hands. What do you do while you are waiting? What does one do, in Richard Bewes's words, in the 'in-between times' of life? Do you get a book, catch up on reading, buy some newspapers and catch up on the news, do you go to the cinema, do you see a play at the West End? Who's pulling your strings? Who's pulling your strings when you are alone? Someone has said that a man tells what he is really like by what he does when he is utterly alone.

Paul was alone, and what was he like? Luke tells us that while he waited at Athens his spirit stirred within him when he saw the idolatry there in the city, verse 16. I've often been attracted to that verse, that one's spirit can be stirred and gripped. It has always reminded me of that verse in Jeremiah when the writer says the word of God was in him like fire in his bones (Jer 20:9). When is the last time you were gripped by the Spirit? When is the last time you were stirred and you knew God was at the bottom of it all? I can't say that this has happened to me many times but it certainly happened when at Westminster Chapel I invited Arthur Blessitt to come and preach (Chapter 8). When Arthur got us out on the streets witnessing, and I saw what could happen on the streets, I began to experience my spirit burning in me and I could only think of those words in Jeremiah, 'a burning fire shot up in my bones' and of this verse where it says, 'While Paul waited for them at Athens, his spirit stirred in him.'

The challenge to be a witness

So what stirred Paul? We are told that his spirit was stirred in him when he saw the city wholly given to idolatry. Now he had not come to Athens to conduct an evangelistic campaign. The Lord Mayor of Athens did not come out to welcome him, the rulers of the synagogue did not invite Paul to conduct a mission, he was only waiting with a little time on his hands. Donald Gray Barnhouse once said, 'While we wait we can worship' but it is also true that while we wait we can witness, and I think that what the Holy Spirit was saying to us in Westminster Chapel those years ago was that there is something we can do while we are waiting. In the past twenty years, the cults, false religions—the Muslims, the Moonies, the Mormons and the Jehovah's Witnesses—have been winning more converts in this country than the church has won, partly because they have been going out onto the streets while we have been waiting comfortably in our pews for God to send them in. I can remember one dear man used to pray every week at our prayer meeting, 'Lord, send in thine elect', but I knew that there was something we must do. Well, what did Paul do? We are told he disputed with those in the synagogue, and he went to the market place daily. In fact, he went and spoke with those that happened to be there.

When is the last time you witnessed to a stranger? How long has it been since you personally led a soul to Jesus Christ? Do you know whether or not your milkman is a Christian? I was not always able to witness but something happened to me. God knew what he had to do to bring me to the place where I would see I wasn't being an evangelist just because I preached evangelistic sermons. I always thought I was doing my job as an evangelist because in the pulpit every Sunday night I would preach the gospel. I thought that was enough; it never crossed my mind that I should have to witness to someone on the train or on the bus, or to anybody I would run into. I just never bothered about that kind of thing, and it's that which we all want least of all to do, for no one becomes a witness under his own steam. We don't like it, God has to box us in, and God put me in a position where I had no choice. So don't get the idea that I'm on a pedestal, believe me it was the last thing I ever wanted to do, to go to the streets and talk to people about Jesus Christ.

I'll tell you, I wasn't the only one who was reluctant to do it. After I began witnessing on the streets my own wife Louise was the last to be convinced. She said it was all right for Arthur to carry his cross around the world and witness to strangers and people on the street, but we didn't have to do anything like that; and she was digging her heels in just a little bit. But one Saturday morning to my surprise she said she was going out with the Pilot Lights today. What I didn't know was that she had asked God for a sign that he was behind what I was doing. In the meantime we had begun 'Evangelism Explosion' in the chapel—that's Jim Kennedy's method of witnessing and leading people to Christ, and I myself took the course. My wife said that she didn't need to take the course. After all, she had been sitting under my preaching for twenty-five years, that should count for something! I had no answer to that.

The day she went out on the streets she hadn't been out thirty minutes witnessing by the St James's Park tube station when a young man, about twenty years old with a Che Guevara T-shirt, walked alongside her, and saw her giving out these tracts. He went up to her and asked her what she was doing. She said, 'I don't suppose you want one of these little tracts?' and he grabbed it saying, 'Sure, let me have it.' It was a little pack called 'What is Christianity?'. He looked at it and tears filled his eyes. He looked at her and he said, 'I'm a Marxist, I'm an atheist, but five minutes ago I was in a church and I just said, "God if you're really there let me run into somebody who believes in you."' He said to her, 'You've got five minutes to convert me, I've got to get a train,' and then she realised how helpless she was. She didn't know what to say. She came back and she enrolled in our EE Programme and she's now a trainer of others.

We've all had to have something happen to make us see it. I think it's often true that a person can sit under preaching and expect something just to happen, but when God gives you every signal and you don't act upon it, you can sit under the greatest preaching in the world, you can go to Spring Harvest or whatever, enjoy the worship, go to the seminars and nothing will happen to you. But when your spirit is stirred it is a time to act, and Paul knew what he had to do. He had time on his hands. He went to the synagogues, he went and spoke to what were called God-fearing Greeks and to the market place.

What had happened was that those who lived in Athens had become almost impervious to everything that had gone on. They lived with the idolatry, and so it hadn't occurred to the people in the synagogues to be too bothered by it—they saw it all the time. So with many of us what we see on television, what we read in the newspapers, becomes second nature to us and we are not aware of how we are being affected by it; but Paul comes into Athens and his spirit is stirred. He probably wasn't very successful in saying much in the synagogues, and so he went to the market place and began to talk with those who happened to be there.

We're told in verse 18 that the Epicureans and the Stoics were there. Now in ancient Judaism there were largely the Pharisees and the Sadducees, but in the ancient Greek philosophical world there were largely the Epicureans and the Stoics. The Epicureans were the existentialists of the day. They were those who said—do your own thing, whatever turns you on, eat, drink and be merry, we have an existence, we were thrown into our existence, we didn't ask to be here, there's no meaning, there's no purpose.

The Stoics were more contemplative, they were the theorists, they were largely followers of Plato. They developed the idea that you should be indifferent to pain and that it was virtue not to show your emotions.

Now it happens that in our day there are two types of modern secular man. There is the pleasure-seeking type, without any serious philosophical rationale, influenced by existentialism but not knowing that that was the cause of it. Then you've got the more intellectual, those who claim to have thought things through. But they all end up in the same way—seeking pleasure. Paul was unafraid of both types, and so he began to talk to them. We are told in verse 18 that he 'preached unto them Jesus, and the resurrection.' Surely not, you would say. If you ever have a chance to talk to someone who is learned, someone who is sophisticated or a typical modern man, you must surely talk about things that interest them and show that you know something about them. Paul simply went and talked to them about Jesus and the resurrection. This is always his method. Here was a man fully capable of talking to them on their level, but he knew he had what they had to have to be saved, and without apology he just went right in and talked to them about Jesus and the resurrection.

What do you suppose was their reaction? They called him a babbler. Paul knew that there was only one way they could be saved, and that was by hearing the gospel. He had to let them know that Jesus died on the cross and was raised from the dead. So he had to make a very important decision when he envisaged going to Corinth.

He knew that Corinth was filled with people, the equivalent of philosophers or professors of Oxford and Cambridge, and he thought, 'What will I do when I go to Corinth? A lot of learned people there, perhaps I'd better read up a little more on Eros, Plato and Socrates so that I can go in there and show them how much I know.' But he said, 'We made a decision before we came, I determined to know nothing among you save Jesus Christ and him crucified.' Don't believe that isn't going to be accepted in Britain today. I can tell you this, if anybody is ever converted it will be because they hear that message, and any kind of confession of faith that was made when they hadn't heard the gospel must always be suspect.

Paul knew there was no God framework in Corinth, and there was certainly no God framework in Athens, and so what did he do when he went to a place where they don't even believe in God?—He preached Jesus. According to 1 Peter 1:21, never think that you can't preach Jesus just because people don't believe in God. They'll not believe in God until they have heard of Jesus who was raised from the dead. And yet most of us would probably be scared to death if we had been accepted as Paul was. They said, 'This man is a babbler.' Don't expect modern man to flatter you or to quote you accurately. Be willing to be misunderstood and misquoted.

But Paul didn't panic when they did not receive him, and his dialogue with them led him to a wider ministry. We're told that these same men took him and brought him on to the Areopagus—it was a most prestigious place to be invited to. I doubt it ever would have crossed Paul's mind that when he got to Athens he would eventually be invited to address these people at the Areopagus. You see we never know what God will do through us if we are simply obedient. When he went to Sunset Strip in Hollywood Arthur Blessitt erected a twelve-foot cross which weighed 90lbs and put it on the wall of his coffee shop to let people who came in know that it was a different place, and there would be no booze but only orange juice and coffee. One day at 5 o'clock in the morning God told him to take the cross down, and carry it on foot around the world. When he began to tell this to his friends they all backed off, they couldn't believe that he was serious. But he did it! He began walking on Christmas day 1969 and now he has carried the cross in over eighty countries. He has been to the North Pole and the South Pole, he has been invited into places that you and I will never get to. No one could have known that because he was obedient, he would address heads of state and speak to governments. He stayed in Prime Minister Begin's home, was given the Sinai peace medal, he spent days with Yasser Arafat, witnessing to the Arabs and Palestinians. This is the impulse of the Spirit—when we can sense our heart strings being pulled from heaven.

The Bible says, 'My Spirit will not always strive with man' (Gen 6:3). A lot of people come to Arthur Blessitt; one lady did and said, 'How is it that God seems to speak to you so clearly? He doesn't speak to me like that.' Arthur just asked her this question, 'Have you ever felt an impulse to witness to somebody you didn't know?' She said, 'yes I have.' He said, 'Begin obeying that impulse, and the voice of the Spirit will be clearer and clearer.' You see, what will happen is that God will speak only so long and then you become stone deaf. Deafness doesn't begin all at once, it's little by little until eventually you can't hear a thing. That's a description of those in Hebrews 6 who had become dull of hearing and finally had reached the place where they couldn't hear God speak at all and couldn't be renewed again unto repentance. So when your spirit is stirred act upon it, or you may never hear him speak again.

What do we say about God?

So it happened that Paul was obedient and the people actually came to him begging: 'May we know please what is this new doctrine that you have?' This was a place where they loved to hear something new, and they spent all their time doing nothing else but telling or hearing some new thing. It almost sounds like a modern theological college. At so many of the colleges today they spend all of their time wanting to discuss what is new, they are so afraid that unless they come up with something new and clever they are not going to reach modern man. The fact is, we are in the same situation today as they were in Athens, there is nothing newer or fresher than this: God sent his Son into the world to die on a cross, he bore our sins and he was raised from the dead. There is nothing more relevant than that, for that is the only way people are going to be saved. So they asked him to address them. Paul took his text from an inscription that he had seen on the way and he said, 'As I passed by, and beheld your devotions, I found an altar with this inscription, TO THE UNKNOWN GOD. Whom therefore ye ignorantly worship, him declare I unto you' (v 23). So Paul put his finger on what Blaise Pascal called 'the God-shaped blank that is in every man' and he touched on their most sensitive points.

First, Paul preached creation by an act of God (17:24). It's amazing to me how people today are so afraid to affirm the creation by an act of God. They say that people today don't believe it; well they didn't believe it then either. The truth is nobody will believe in creation by an act of God except by faith. The writer of Hebrews tells us that nobody by nature believes in creation (Heb 11:3). He didn't say by science we understand. A lot of Christians today are intimidated by science and they're waiting for science finally to come up with something that will encourage them in believing in creation by God. It may be that science will do that. It wouldn't surprise me if science comes to the place where, though they may not become Christians, they will admit they can't explain it. There are more scientists today disillusioned by the traditional views of evolution, and many are throwing up their hands saying they don't understand! But they're not going to come to creation as an act of God except by faith.

Every generation has its stigma by which the believer's faith is tested. In Paul's day the stigma was to believe in the resurrection of Jesus. In the day of Athanasius the stigma was to believe that Jesus was God, Athanasius was in a minority here. A man by the name of Arius was having his way and many were taking Arius seriously. Arius taught that Jesus was simply the highest of God's creations. Athanasius thundered, he is the very God with God, co-equal with the Father, but Athanasius was outnumbered. We have seen before (Chapter 6) that Athanasius was more concerned with truth than popularity when he retorted, 'If the world is against Athanasius, then Athanasius is against the world', and that was the stigma of the day.

If you were living in the sixteenth century the stigma was to believe that you are saved by faith alone. What's the stigma of the twentieth century? Perhaps there is more than one, not the least of which is to affirm that God made everything according to his will. By an act of God, 'things which are seen were not made of things which do appear' (Heb 11:3).

The second thing Paul preached was an historical literal Adam, the first man (17:26). Whenever you accept the theory of evolution you deny the first man and also the New Testament teaching that the whole human race fell by the disobedience of one man. There is far more at stake than you may have thought when you began to cower to the spirit of the age, for the whole purpose and plan of redemption is at issue here.

The third thing Paul taught was that this God whom they ignorantly worshipped was a personal God who decided when and where men should live. Perhaps you thought that your being in this world was an accident. Maybe you feel that there is no purpose in your being where you are and you wonder why you were born in the twentieth century, not the tenth or the third or 1000BC. Why were you born in one country and not another? Paul will give you the answer to that. God had you in mind from the foundation of the world. As Augustine put it, 'God loves every man as though there were no one else to love.' You may think that God misfired when it came to you: not so, you are in his heart. How precious, O Lord, are your thoughts toward me, like the sand of the seashore (see Ps 139:17–18).

The fourth thing is that this God is the one who wanted to have fellowship with man. Paul said the reason that God made man is 'that they should seek the Lord, if haply they might feel after him, and find him, though he be not far from every one of us: For in him we live, and move, and have our being; as certain also of your own poets have said, for we are also his offspring.' Perhaps you feel that God is breathing down your neck and sometimes you've actually said, 'God leave me alone!' Why does God breathe down your neck? Why is he there? Why is it that though you are running from him he stays with you? I marvel at God's patience with me. I don't know why he has stayed with me. I have grieved him by a thousand falls but he is the God who wants to have fellowship with me.

There is another thing about this God. As Paul says, he is the God who demands repentance. For 'the times of this ignorance God winked at; but now commandeth all men every where to repent' (17:30). Now Paul is beginning to come to the bottom line in saying something about this God. Not only that he is Creator, not only that he has made us and planned our lives and wants fellowship with us, but that he is a holy God. Thrice holy and demanding repentance. We must change our ways. We do men no favour to withhold from them this, that God hates sin. Maybe you're one of those who like to live on the edge of danger, just to see how close you can get, but if you began to see how much God hates sin you would run from it. You could understand why the first message of the New Testament by John the Baptist was 'Flee from the wrath to come' (Mt 3:7). This is the last thing Paul says, 'Because he has appointed a day in which he will judge the world.'

I wonder if you are aware of why it is that we must repent. Is it because we are going to feel better? Well, we will. Is it because it will make us better? Certainly it will. But when all is said and done, what is the real reason we are required to repent? Because God has appointed a day in which he will judge the world. We are all going to have to stand before God and you are going to have to give an account of how you have lived your life, how you have spent your time. What you've done with that body God has given you, the temple of the Holy Spirit. A lot of people think the reason you become a Christian is simply because you are going to be better off in this life, and I don't doubt that that is true, you will be. But you know there is a sentimental idea which I have been hearing for years—people say, 'Well if there were no hell or no heaven I'd still be a Christian.' I know what they mean by that, but you see Paul would never talk like that. He said if there's no heaven there's no hell. We in this life are men most miserable, it's not worth it. Why are we to call people to repent? Why does God call you to repent? Because there is a day, the point to which all history is moving. The Old Testament prophets called it 'the Day of the Lord'; it is sometimes called 'a Day'; it is sometimes called 'the Day', but that final judgement will be conducted by none other than Jesus Christ of Nazareth. For he said, as he came to the conclusion of the Sermon on the Mount, 'They will come and say unto me in that day, Lord, Lord, have we not done many works in your name? Have we not in your name prophesied? Have we not in your name cast out devils?' (Mt 7:21–22). Why were they saying that to Jesus? It's because they could see that he was getting ready to say to them, 'Depart, I never knew you.' And so as he was getting ready to pronounce the sentence on them they were beginning to say, 'Wait! Stop! Lord, wait just a minute, you forgot the things I did. You have forgotten what I have done, I've done a lot of good things.' It will be an awful day and it will be the day on which God clears his name.

The first question we get asked on the streets when we begin to talk to people about the Lord is, 'If there is a God why does he allow these things to happen to me? Why do the righteous suffer? Why does he allow evil?' and you wonder how God is going to clear his name. Well, I don't know how, but I know that he will. Our omniscient sovereign God in the last day will clear his name and all will see, but it will be too late then. John said, 'Behold he cometh with clouds; and every eye shall see him, and they also which pierced him: and all the kindreds of the earth shall wail because of him' (Rev 1:7), and on that day God will clear his name, but for those who wait until then to see God vindicated they will be lost.

Maybe you say you don't believe in hell. One philosopher said that God is nothing more than man's projection upon the backdrop of the universe, the idea being that we all want to believe a God is there, we want to believe there is a God who takes care, we want to believe that God is going to give us heaven some day, so we project upon the backdrop of the universe that there is a God. I ask who would have thought of hell? Where did that idea come from? Man would have never thought of it. It's God's idea. I don't understand it, but we must lower our voices and remember the question of Abraham, 'Will not the judge of all the earth do right?' It is only for us now to look to God and say, 'Lord thank you that you have been patient with me and you're still speaking to me.'

We might wish that all those learned men at the Areopagus were converted. But no, Paul wasn't eminently successful with them. We're told in verse 32 there were three reactions. Some mocked, some said, 'let

me think about it', but some believed. Only a handful—
not a lot compared with the 3,000 who were converted
when Peter preached on the day of Pentecost; but these
two would not have been converted at all had not Paul's
spirit been set on fire when he came to Athens, had not
the Holy Spirit pulled his heart strings when he was in
the inbetween times. You may take to the streets and not
see thousands saved, but if anybody at all is converted—
and God will give you some—they are worth everything!

Chapter 12

Ready to Witness

ACTS 26

We are looking at the apostle Paul testifying before King Agrippa. 'For it is not ye that speak, but the Spirit of your Father which speaketh in you' (Mt 10:20). I think that this applies to all the cases that we have been looking at. For example, in Acts 2, I doubt that Peter had time to prepare a sermon. I'm sure it was much the same for Stephen before the Sanhedrin, Paul before the Areopagus, and so also in this case. Paul was just giving his testimony.

There are at least four kinds of apologetics. First, that which is defended spontaneously. Secondly, that which has been thought out through careful study. In the early church God raised up men like Irenaeus who combated Gnosticism. Thomas Aquinas was the great apologist of the Middle Ages, famous for his cosmological proofs of God, and Anselm, Archbishop of Canterbury was famous for his ontological proof of God. In our generation there are men like Carl Henry, and the late Francis Schaeffer.

There is a third kind of apologetics. Some would plausibly argue that faith is defended by a demonstration of the Spirit and one hopes and prays for more of this, that which defies a natural explanation. Not that everybody will become Christians if they see the Spirit demonstrated in great power, for that certainly didn't happen in the New Testament, but then neither does it always happen with the other kinds of apologetics.

The fourth kind of apologetics is personal testimony. Many times, nothing is more powerful than one's own testimony, and that is what we are looking at now. We are looking at a fulfilment of Jesus' own words in Matthew 10:18, 'Ye shall be brought before governors and kings for my sake, for a testimony against them and the Gentiles.' This was happening with Paul before Agrippa. In fact, it was a fulfilment of God's word to Ananias, because in Acts 9 when Ananias said of Paul, 'Lord I've heard many things about this man, the evil that he has done', God told him that Paul would bear Jesus' name before kings. The day has come, Paul is before a king.

It's a culmination of a series of events which actually began in chapter 21. Certain people tried to persuade Paul not to go to Jerusalem, but Paul insisted and sure enough he got into trouble. He was eventually put into prison in Caesarea. Paul in the meantime insisted on being tried by the Roman authorities; after all he was a Roman citizen. Festus the Governor had said, 'You have appealed to Caesar, to Caesar you will go.' But in the meanwhile Festus told King Agrippa about Paul. The King was curious, fascinated. No doubt he had heard of Paul and wanted to meet him. So he asks here for Paul's account and the moment has arrived, Paul's moment to speak before a king. We've seen him in the market place, we saw him at the Areopagus, but now before a king.

What does a man say to a king? Who's pulling your strings when you're in the presence of royalty? You will say, 'That will never happen to me, that leaves me out. I don't need to worry about that.' Jesus said, 'He that is faithful in that which is least is faithful also in much' (Lk 16:10), and if you are a witness all the time to those who know you, you have no idea what God might do and what hearing he might give you. But if we are not witnesses in the smaller areas of life we will not be ready when the greater moment arrives. The question could be this—would Paul change his tune and change his message once he got before a king? It's one thing to be faithful when you are in the world or talking to Christians or speaking with those who already believe, but what do you do when you are in the presence of such enormous power? Paul was the same as he had always been. He wanted to see King Agrippa converted. He wasn't the slightest bit interested in himself or preserving his own life. He had known for years that the day would come. He knew what God had said to Ananias. This is the moment and Paul knows he has got one chance to lead a king to Christ. So he is not interested in defending himself, he said as is recorded back in chapter 21:13, 'I am ready not to be bound only, but also to die at Jerusalem for the name of the Lord Jesus.'

How do we know that Paul was actually trying to convert Agrippa? It is so often said that it doesn't matter if you convert them just so long as you pray for them. But we know by Agrippa's own comment, for after Festus had lost his temper and ended Paul's testimony, Paul turned to Agrippa and said, 'Do you believe the prophets, King Agrippa? I know you do.' Then Agrippa spoke up and said, 'Paul, did you really think in such a short period of time you can turn me into a Christian?' Paul certainly did think he could do it. Away with the nonsense that there must be a long time of preparation before a person can be converted. One of the things about going on the streets in Westminster on Saturdays is that our Pilot Lights are trained to lead people to Christ right on the spot. In the old days the most you ever thought of doing was to invite them to church or give them a tract, but if you set as a goal to give a tract away that is all you will ever accomplish. Who knows, you might lead them to Christ. Give them gospel, aim high, you might see some saved.

The right approach

However, one of the first things that we notice as Paul begins his testimony is the respect that he shows to the king. When Paul spoke he said he was honoured to be there and showed a great deal of respect. There is a right way and a wrong way to witness. For example, if you do work at Buckingham Palace I don't suggest that you slap a Jesus sticker on the Duke of Edinburgh! What Paul does then, having shown this respect for the king, is to begin with his own background. Why does he do that? Partly to introduce himself and partly to show that he himself was now aware how wrong he once was. This is something that is always disarming, when we admit how right we thought we were and we had to come to see that we were wrong. Before his conversion Paul never thought that there was much wrong with him. Proverbs 14:12 says, 'There is a way which seemeth right unto a man, but the end thereof are the ways of death.'

Paul said three things at this stage, first to show how religious one can think one is when the real problem is one of unbelief (26:4–5).

Secondly, to show how righteous one can think one is when the real problem is one of sin (26:9). It may be you feel quite righteous in yourself, perhaps because you are moral. The Bible says that our righteousness is as filthy rags in God's sight. If you only knew how much God hates self-righteousness. When you see that, you will see how sinful your righteousness is in God's sight.

Thirdly, to show how brilliant one can think one is when the real problem is one of ignorance. And so he says in verse 10, which Paul discusses when he writes his letter to Timothy, 'Who was before a blasphemer, and a persecutor, and injurious: but I obtained mercy, because I did it ignorantly in unbelief' (1 Tim 1:12). I have always been gripped by those words 'I obtained mercy.' You see Paul could never forget the way God saved him. Never in a thousand years could he take the slightest credit for what had happened to him. He could only explain what happened to him in terms of God alone. So he led the rest of his life conscious that he had obtained mercy. But he went on to say that his own conversion was a pattern to those who should believe thereafter. That is a way of saying that all of us are in the same situation. If God could save Paul he could save anybody, and if God can save you he can save anybody. We have one explanation for being Christians today, it is by the sheer grace of God, mercy, that quality which can be given or withheld and justice be done in either case.

Paul is conveying, 'I obtained mercy', and so it is in that spirit he tells his story to King Agrippa. He has probably told it by now a hundred times, but it was fresh every time he told it. Paul just never got over being saved. He could never forget that on the day he was saved he was not on his way to an evangelistic campaign, he wasn't on his way to investigate the claims of Christianity to see if they might be right. He knew what he was trying to do. He was on his way to Damascas to get more authority to kill more Christians. What happened to him defied a natural explanation as Paul would later say to the Ephesians, 'by grace are ye saved through faith; and that not of yourselves: it is the gift of God: Not of works, lest any man should boast' (Eph 2:8–9). So Paul says here, 'O King, I saw a brightness more brilliant than the noonday sun, it blazed all around me and my companions. We fell to the ground and I heard a voice, it was the voice of Jesus— Saul, Saul, why do you persecute me?' (26:13–14). For Paul found out that persecuting the church was perse- cuting Jesus, and that proved Jesus was alive. But that's not all. In that same encounter, Paul says to Agrippa, God gave him a mission (26:16–17). Why would Paul tell this to Agrippa? He was doing it to show partly that Christians were not troublemakers, but he also wanted Agrippa to know that every person who was converted to Jesus Christ was also given a mission to accomplish.

God gives to every person that he has saved a gift. We all have our place and there is something that we can do that nobody else can do as well. Paul is saying to Agrippa that this was what God told him to do. And now he could say, 'I was not disobedient unto the heavenly vision' (26:19), so all that had happened to him was the consequence of what God did and what God told him to do.

The right content

So Paul wanted Agrippa to see what a Christian was and he listed five things. Firstly, a Christian is a person who sees with a new set of eyes (26:18).

Secondly, a Christian is a person who has been delivered from Satan's dominion. Never forget this, that when you are talking to another person about Jesus Christ, not only is he by nature dead in tresspasses and sins, but the god of this world, Satan, has blinded him lest he see the light of the knowledge of the glory of God in the face of Jesus Christ.

Third, forgiveness of sins. A Christian is a person who knows that he is forgiven. It's a marvellous feeling, there is nothing to compare with it, that all of my sins are washed away. 'As far as the east is from the west, so far hath he removed our transgressions from us' (Ps 103:12). What a marvellous feeling, to feel clean and to know that your sins are washed away by Jesus' blood.

Fourth, a new inheritance—'that they may receive forgiveness of sins, an inheritance among them which are sanctified by faith that is in me' (26:18). It's a marvellous thing to know that you are saved by faith alone. Not on the condition that you will be a certain kind of person, but on the condition that you put all of your eggs into one basket—that Jesus paid your debt on the cross. Yet the person who has that trust will be changed and he will know that those who are in Christ are a new creation. We know we are saved, not because we are good enough but because Jesus paid our debt.

We are saved by transferring the trust that we have in ourselves by nature to what Jesus did for us on the cross. It is not arrogant to say that you are going to heaven. We are often accused by people, 'You must really be a wonderful person. I wouldn't say that I could go to heaven,' because everybody by nature thinks that is how you get to heaven, by being good. Not at all. It is the awareness that Jesus paid your debt and it is God's integrity at stake. I am trusting his word so I know I'm going to heaven, not because of anything in me but because Jesus paid my debt on the cross.

That is not all that Paul reminded Agrippa of. Because when God said to him, 'Stand on your feet,' he said he was going to make Paul a witness of the things he had seen but also of things which were going to happen to Paul in the future. Conversion isn't the last time God speaks to you. When you are first converted God doesn't say, 'Well, it's good to know you, I'll see you in heaven. I won't be talking to you any more because I've got other things to do and other people to save, so see you in heaven.' No, the things which you have seen and the things which will be shown to you in the future. When is the last time God showed you something? God speaks continually with us and you should be conscious of being changed from glory to glory, even as by the Spirit of the Lord. Then you have new depths of insight and God is real to you.

Fifthly, Paul proceeded to show in what way he was obedient. He says in verse 20 the very first thing he did was that he wanted to witness to those in Damascus. It's as though he went to them and said, 'You remember I was supposed to show up the other day, well a funny thing happened to me on the way. ...' Then he went next to Jerusalem, then Judaea and then to the Gentiles and then he says in his defence, 'I have preached nothing but what Moses and the prophets said would happen.' Namely this, that the Messiah, the Lord's Christ would die but he would be raised from the dead and that he would be offered to the Gentiles; and this was the point where Festus lost his temper. Festus was the Roman Governor, Festus was a Gentile and the moment Paul mentioned Gentiles, Festus stopped the whole thing and said, 'Paul, you are beside yourself. All of your learning has driven you to insanity.'

'Not at all,' says Paul. 'What I'm saying is both true and reasonable.' As he had said back in verse 8, 'Why should it be thought a thing incredible with you, that God should raise the dead?', that's a reasonable thing for God to do.

And he says, 'The King here knows exactly what I'm talking about' and then Paul turned to Agrippa, 'Do you believe the prophets? I know you do.'

This is when Agrippa said, 'Do you think, short time or long, that you can persuade me?'

And Paul says, 'I pray God, no matter how long it takes, that not only you but all who are listening to me today should become what I am except for these chains.'

There's something here that is very sad. Agrippa has condemned himself. He has plainly told us now that he is not a Christian, despite Paul's pleadings. It shows also as a reminder for anybody that believing the prophets or certain things in the Bible is not the same thing as believing the gospel, for obviously King Agrippa believed some of the Old Testament but when he heard the gospel he said, 'No thanks.' And so it is a reminder to people who say, 'Well I believe in the Bible, I believe that Jesus was a good man' and things like that. The devil believes in one God and trembles. The fact that some people believe in God and believe something in the Bible proves nothing. Maybe they've called on God to help them when they were in trouble. General McArthur used to say, 'There are no atheists in fox holes' (trenches). Six years ago in the Falklands War I heard reports of British soldiers everywhere becoming Christians. Where are most of them today? What Paul is saying here to Agrippa, whatever else is implied, is that there is a need for a commitment. That is what Paul was wanting to see accomplished. The Authorised Version quotes Agrippa as saying, 'Almost thou persuadest me to be a Christian.' Well I think Agrippa was almost persuaded. We sing a hymn back in the hills of Kentucky called 'Almost Persuaded', but there is that one line in it: 'Almost, but lost.'

The result of witnessing

How many are like that—almost a Christian but lost? Paul finished his testimony. He poured his heart out, this was his moment he had been waiting for for years, to get to witness to a king. He watched every expression on Agrippa's face, and the time came when he was taken with his chains back to his cell. Oh, how much he would want some kind of positive feed-back. Did Agrippa get saved? Was he moved? Others may have asked, 'I wonder what he thought when he heard Paul testify.' It's all so sad. So lack-lustre, so anticlimactic. If only Agrippa had made a comment directly about what Paul actually said. There was a comment, only one comment, and this is the way the chapter ends, the only thing Agrippa said having heard Paul preach, 'This man might have been set at liberty, if he had not appealed unto Caesar' (26:32). He was overheard saying that to Festus.

His final word. After all this, something that Paul looked forward to so much. I'm sure that Paul envisaged that God would have told Ananias years ago that one day he would testify before a king because the King was going to be saved. It would be a reasonable conclusion. It may be that you have gone to a lot of preparation for a particular meeting and you have felt the presence of the Lord and everything was falling into place and you just knew God was going to work, and then the moment comes and you don't see much happen and you think,

'What was it all for?' I quote an old friend, Henry Mahan from Ashland, Kentucky, who always used to say, 'If the pure gospel is preached to men as they are, it will save some and condemn others, but will accomplish God's purpose.' In Agrippa's only comment he was just speaking in an indifferent, matter-of-fact way. 'Good chap this man Paul, he doesn't do anything wrong, he could have been set free if he hadn't appealed to Caesar.' How do you suppose that made Paul feel? He wasn't wanting to be vindicated, he wanted to see Agrippa saved!

Maybe you know the feeling. I know what it is to preach my heart out and know that I've said something important. I remember preaching once in Fort Lauderdale. There was a man in the service I was so glad was there. The whole time I was preaching I was thinking of him. I felt unusual power and couldn't wait to get his reaction at the doorway. He patted me on the shoulder and said, 'Hey R T, I like to hear you talk, you're really good.' But that was all there was.

I once had the privilege of speaking to a man, a Jew from Miami Beach and the founder of Pepsi Cola. I got to know him quite well. One evening I was going over Isaiah 53 with him and I thought, 'This is going to happen,' as I was showing him Jesus in Isaiah 53. I came to verse 6, 'the Lord hath laid on him the iniquity of us all.' He was just looking right at me and I thought, 'Praise the Lord, it's happening,' and he said, 'You're terrific, you're terrific. You ought to be on television. You're great!' 'Oh no,' I thought, 'he doesn't hear a thing I'm saying!'

And so Paul witnesses to Agrippa. 'This man could have been set free,' that's the climax. But our best defence may not convert people and our testimony though filled with the Spirit may not convert them. Some will be saved, others condemned, but God's purpose will be accomplished.

PART FOUR

DECKCHAIRS ON THE TITANIC

(Resisting the Enemy)

Chapter 13

God's Plan in Adversity

I wonder if you have to live where you would not naturally have chosen to live? I wonder if you have to work where you would not have chosen to work? Or live with people you would not have chosen to live with? Now if you are doing all these things according to your choice, it is wonderful and you should be very thankful and praise the Lord for it. But if you are having to do things you would not have chosen to do then the book of Daniel generally and this chapter particularly is of special relevance to you.

In the early verses of Daniel 1 we are told how a few young men came from the privileged class in Jerusalem and came to be in Babylon before the first deportation of the Israelies in 597BC. If you know the book of Jeremiah you will know that Jeremiah the prophet warned of the coming Babylonian captivity, nobody believed him then but now it was a fact. These four men were taken in advance of the rest of the Israelies who would soon be in Babylon. They could only be called hostages and they were from the Judean aristocracy. Their going there would only weaken the forces back in Israel. It perhaps is the first recorded example of what we now call 'the brain drain', except that today, whereas some of the better minds choose to live elsewhere, these hostages were having to leave and being forced to live in an alien country and culture, to be useful to their conqueror in Babylon.

So these young men were brought to the Royal Court in Babylon. They were living where they would not have chosen, they were having to learn things they would not have chosen to learn. They were having to learn a new language, literature of a new culture was forced upon them, and they were with people and doing things they would not have chosen.

Now it would seem that the choice of these hostages was made partly on the basis of their good looks, physical perfection and intelligence: 'Then the King ordered Ashpenaz, chief of his court officials, to bring in some of the Israelites from the royal family and the nobility—young men without any physical defect, handsome, showing aptitude for every kind of learning, well informed, quick to understand, and qualified to serve in the king's palace' (1:3–4). In other words they were unlucky in being good-looking and clever. They were also passive victims of a previous generation's disobedience. It may have seemed unfair that they were suffering the judgement of God upon their nation, when they themselves were not of the generation that had incurred the wrath of God, but the truth is that Israel was under the judgement of God. I believe that this is of particular relevance for all of us because it seems to me that the church, speaking generally, is under God's judgement. But God had not forsaken Israel and nor is he forsaking his church. Jeremiah prophesied of the captivity and said that it would last seventy years, so that one day the people of Israel would return to their own land. The events described in the book of Daniel took place during those seventy years, and what we have in chapter 1 is what it was like at the very beginning of that captivity. So that the first to arrive were these four men from the Judean aristocracy. All those who were carried away had to settle in a country, a climate and a culture not their own.

Now the book of Daniel among other things is a

demonstration of how God protects, preserves, defends and prepares his own. If I were to have to come up with one word that would describe the thrust of these four chapters that we are examining it is the word vindication.

Do you know what it is to be vindicated? It is to be cleared after having been falsely accused. It is to have your name cleared. To be cleared of blame or suspicion. I doubt that there is anything more painful than being unvindicated, when you have taken a stand in a particular situation and no one agrees with you. Do you know the pain of having people distance themselves from you?

But the theme of the book of Daniel is the theme of vindication. And it is a description of how those who were unafraid to stand up and be counted were in the end vindicated. They were cleared and even exalted.

So here we are looking at these four men who were caught in the conflict between Babylonian imperialism and the claims of their God. The book of Daniel also shows how God can place his people in strategic places of influence and power. Often at times a person will be exalted and have a place of influence, but then when he gets that influence he is not the person he was. I've known a lot of people who longed for the day they would have a platform or be in a position to influence a broader number of people, who say, 'If I ever get there here is what I'm going to do. ...' Then once they get there they have been through so many compromises and change in the meantime, that though they are in that position, they cease to have a real voice. I hope that there might be some reading this who have the conviction that one day God is going to use you; the question is whether you will be equal to that occasion because you still are the man or woman that you were when God burned in your heart that some day you would have a voice. It is a very sad thing to watch a person come up through the ranks only to find that by the time he is in a place of power he has no message.

But here were four men who got to the place of

influence and power, and found that they had not compromised. They knew what their responsibility was and they carried it out. So here is a word of terrific encouragement today, a demonstration of how the church can be under the judgement of God generally, and yet how a few select individuals may nonetheless see God work very powerfully indeed.

Using your gifts

What do we know about these four men? We know that they were valuable men. They were as I have said from Judah's aristocracy. Their gifts were traceable to what some theologians would call common grace. This is a Calvinistic concept, the idea being that all men are given common grace, that is, grace common to all. It is distinct from 'saving grace'. Saving grace is when a person is given saving faith and it transfers the trust that he had in his good works to what Jesus did on the cross. A person is saved when he knows he has no claim upon God except through the merit of Jesus Christ. When we believe that, it is called 'saving grace'.

But common grace is God's favour to all men, whether or not they are converted. It is what comes at the level of nature by virtue of creation, so that all of us have been given a measure of common grace. Any ability you have is there because God gave it to you through the endowment of creation. Your IQ is what God gave you. When you become a Christian the chances are that your IQ will not be elevated one bit— you will still be what you are. You may have a great ability to play the violin or play the organ, or to speak publicly, these are gifts that come at the natural level.

Of course a lot of people are endowed with a great measure of common grace and never come to Jesus Christ and we have known of great men in the world raised up by God, the Einsteins of this world, or people like Rachmaninov, Tchaikovsky, or Yehudi Menuhin.

God gave these gifts and these gifted men but it is not because they were Christians. Yet when there is that element of common grace given to the church it is a wonderful thing, when there is a coinciding of common grace and saving grace. When God gives the world an Augustine, or an Athanasius, a Luther, a Calvin, a Whitefield, a Wesley, a Spurgeon, a Martyn Lloyd-Jones. When those things overlap it is a wonderful thing indeed.

The men in Daniel were valuable men who had great gifts, but they also knew that to whom much is given shall much be required. And they knew that they would become useless to God if they deserted him. And yet these were victimised men. They didn't ask to be where they were. Perhaps they were tempted to a bit of self-pity. Maybe they asked the question, 'Why me? Why must I be chosen to live in Babylon?' Do you know what it is like to live where you may not have chosen to live but you also realise that God has you there because the truth is that if you were living where you would have chosen to live, perhaps you wouldn't amount to what you will amount to under God?

I remember a few years ago when my wife and I were on holiday in the Florida Keys, our favourite place in the world really. I was saying goodbye to my friend, Bruce Porter. He was pastor of a church nestled in the heart of the Keys and we were having to go back to London. I said, 'Bruce, you lucky man,' as we were standing in the warm balmy breezes, the coconut palms swaying gently, 'Bruce, you get to live here.'

'You know, I'd rather live in North Carolina,' he said.

The next day I went to Fort Lauderdale just before leaving for London and met my friend O S Hawkins from the First Baptist Church there. I said, 'O S, look at this sunset, look at these palm trees, you lucky man you get to live here.'

He said, 'I'd rather live in Texas.'

And it hit me, the reason Bruce Porter was used of God is that he isn't where he wanted to live. If I were living in the Florida Keys I would want to spend all of my time fishing and I am sure I wouldn't amount to a whole lot. And so with O S, he is not a fisherman. God is using him powerfully in Fort Lauderdale, fishing for men.

These four men would never have been known had they stayed back in Jerusalem. God may have put you in a particular place where you think, 'Why do I have to live here?' But God knows what he is up to. You may ask why you are on a particular course at the moment and it is being required of you to learn things you feel you do not need. We are told that these four men had to learn another language as well as the literature of the Babylonians. That is the last thing they wanted to do. I could only think of something that happened to me some years ago when I was a pastor of a church in Fort Lauderdale in Florida, and I felt led to return to university because I hadn't finished. It was burning on my heart to do this, but I thought, 'why should I go back to university? I can preach, I was brought up in a Christian home, I know the Bible fairly well, why should I go back to university?' It happened in the providence of God that we went to Colorado for the annual Southern Baptist Convention and I could think of almost nothing else but having to return to university and seminary. At the time I was about thirty-five years of age and I knew if I did everything that I felt I would have to do I would be forty years old by the time I had finished, and I thought these would be five wasted years—why should I go back to university when the world is going to hell? I need to be out soul-winning. And yet I couldn't think of anything else and I had no peace.

While in Denver, Colorado, I was high up in the gallery listening to the sermon when suddenly I just got tuned out and I was almost in another realm. I said, 'Lord, if you are really leading me to go back to university, I have to have you speak.' What I did that day I am quite serious when I say I don't recommend that you do. I had a little New Testament and I know the

danger of opening your Bible at anything and claiming
it to be a word from God. I said, 'God if you are in this
I've got to have a word that makes me know so un-
mistakably that I'll never doubt this is really of you. And
I know you can do it—just one time show me in your
word.' And you know as I took my Bible, my heart was
almost pounding out of my chest because it was one of
those moments I knew I was going to get spoken to. I
opened it to Acts 7:22–23 and it read, 'Moses was
educated in all the wisdom of the Egyptians ... When
Moses was forty years old, he decided to visit his fellow
Israelites.' Here were the two things that I had com-
plained about the most. Firstly I would be forty by the
time I would really begin to be a minister, and secondly
why would I need to learn things that I thought wouldn't
relate to preaching? But Moses was learned in all the
wisdom of the Egyptians and when he was forty God was
then ready to use him. Spurgeon said, 'If I knew I had
twenty-five years left to live I would spend twenty of
them in preparation.'

You may feel that what you are having to learn is
needless, but you see any learning is good for the
clearing and the training of the mind. You may feel that
Bible study is unnecessary. You may feel that having to
listen to sermons is something irrelevant, but I have to
tell you that I am distressed by a trend I see at the
moment where people are getting carried away with
nothing but worship and feel there is no time for the exposition of the Scriptures. I address you on bended knee if
you are in a position of leadership, because you need to
see the priority of Bible study, of teaching, of preaching.
It has been put like this (it is not original with me):

> All worship and we burn up,
> All teaching and we dry up,
> The right balance, we grow up.

Making a stand

Yet the way these four men were being victimised was taken a stage further: not only were they having to engage in new learning in a new and strange culture—we are told they were given new names. And so to Daniel was given the name Belteshazzar; to Hananiah, Shadrach; to Mishael, Meshach; and to Azariah, Abednego. So we will be learning about Shadrach, Meshach and Abednego. I don't know whether you could remember those names but there were some kids at Sunday School in Westminster Chapel who called them Your-shack, My-shack and A-bungalow. It is very painful though to have to go by a name you are not used to, and we all know what we want to be called.

These four men also had the uncomfortable stigma of being foreign. We all have our racial, national and cultural prejudices. We all have them, we all feel that our background is the best, our nationality is the right one. A song by Flanders and Swann illustrates this:

It is not that they're wicked or naturally bad
It is knowing they're foreign that makes them so mad
The English, the English, the English are best
I wouldn't give tuppence for all of the rest

They were virtuous men. That is they had some personal conviction. Moral excellence was theirs, and they were willing to accept the new culture, the new climate, the new country. They were even going to be called by names they weren't used to. But there was one thing where they resolved to be different. In verse 8 it says, 'Daniel resolved not to defile himself with the royal food and wine, and he asked the chief official for permission not to defile himself in this way.' I don't know what the food was—I would have thought that it would be the only thing about the new culture that would be good! It would be marvellous to live in a strange country and get to live on caviar, smoked salmon or whatever it was, I can't imagine rejecting food like that. If you're like me you like all food that isn't good for you. Why, if I were to have my last meal I would want Tandoori king prawns in garlic butter. But you see these men knew what they wanted to eat, and the royal food and wine didn't cohere with the Levitical law of eating. They asked for a diet change (1:12). Now according to one world authority on fibre in diet, Daniel's pulse and water was the first recorded high-fibre diet! It would seem they were vegetarians too.

Daniel's diet was apparently edible seeds of peas, beans and lentils. This is going to please all of you vegetarians but that reminds me of Arthur Blessitt's favourite story about the man who said he did not need to witness for Jesus Christ by his words, he would do it by his life. Now, I hear this all the time. There was a man in Los Angeles who was going to witness through his life.

He was on this particular job and after twelve years somebody came up to him and said, 'You know John I have been watching you. You are different.'

And John thought it was beginning to pay off.

'John, let me ask you a question,' he said.

'Sure, you just ask me anything you like,' John said.

'Well, let me just put it to you—there is something different about you. John, are you a vegetarian?'

Well, that is what Shadrach, Meshach and Abednego asked for, but in this they wanted to be true to themselves. They could adjust to the new culture, climate, country, the literature of the learning and even the new names, but on this they said no. My favourite verse in this particular connection is 1 Corinthians 10:13, 'God is faithful, he will not let you be tempted beyond what you can bear.' In the words of one author, 'God will never promote you to the level of your incompetence.' A famous bestseller on both sides of the Atlantic fifteen years ago was called *The Peter Principle*. The thesis of the book was that every man is promoted to the level of his incompetence, so that wherever a person is, the chances are he shouldn't be there, he should have stayed where he was. He has now been given a job where he can't really cope but he won't admit it. He wanted the rise in pay, he wanted the more prestigious position. The author said this was why cars break down because some of the people on the assembly line should have been sweeping floors instead of doing their job. Meanwhile people in office management should have been on the assembly line. Whether it was in the church or politics or in offices, everybody had been promoted to the level of their incompetence.

But God will never promote you to the level of your incompetence. If you will do that which gives you peace, even though it may not get the rise in pay of that prestigious position, if you are true to yourself and you have the courage to be yourself, you will not be mentally exhausted, you won't have fatigue.

What could be the equivalent of the royal food and wine to you? Maybe you are not bothered at all about eating but there is that which you know the Holy Spirit has put his finger on, because of what he has said in his word. Must you resolve not to defile yourself with sex outside of marriage? Or vindicating yourself? Holding that grudge and being filled with bitterness? Self-pity, being judgemental, or is it perhaps the bigger home, the faster car, getting that job or that prestigious invitation?

Daniel, Shadrach, Meshach and Abednego became vulnerable men, that is they put themselves on the line and became liable to be exposed and hurt and embarrassed. But here is the way they put it: 'Please test your servants for ten days, give us nothing but vegetables to eat and water to drink, then compare our appearance with that of the young men who eat the royal food, and treat your servants in accordance with what you see.' So he agreed to this and tested them for ten days.

It is a very vulnerable thing to do, to be true to yourself, true to your convictions and true to the gift

God gave you. A lot of people get themselves into trouble because they will not live within the gift they have and they won't live within the convictions God gave them, but in trying to please people they elevate themselves to a particular level and they do not realise how ridiculous they are. A lot of young Christians want to mimic older Christians, a lot of young ministers want to mimic older ministers, and yet I think it is one of the most difficult things in the world just to be oneself.

You may feel that your gift isn't enough and the conviction you have that you know the Holy Spirit isn't enough either. You may feel that they are not going to put you in good stead. Perhaps you are a teenager and you are having to take your stand in a particular situation. You know how other people are more popular, other kids are getting the invitations and seen with the important people, and you feel it is not worth it.

When I was in High School in Kentucky, I was brought up in a strict Christian home, so I couldn't do what other kids did; and therefore I wasn't in the main clubs and I remember what an inferiority complex I had. They would always have what they call the High School Annuals, a little book with all the pictures of the popular students, and the King of the Prom, the Queen of the Prom, the Captains of the basketball team and football team would all get a full page picture. They had a big picture, I remember, of the person most likely to succeed, and if you go and look up the Annual from my High School you can find my picture; it is there with a group of about fifty people; I'm on the third row, fourth from the end ... if you look really carefully you can find me. I had such a huge inferiority complex in those days.

But not too many years ago I went back, some twenty-five years later, and I said, 'Where is so and so?'

'Oh, him, well you can see him, you'll find him in his house out on the edge of town, sipping vodka in a drunken state. His wife has left him, he can't get a job, he is an alcoholic, no one has anything to do with him.'

That man had been the star basketball player of the district and no one would have dreamed of that happening to him.

I said, 'Well, what about so and so?'

'Oh him, he can't even come to the town now. People are looking for him, he can't even set foot in the city limits.'

There is a saying we have in the hills of Kentucky, 'Don't tell the score in the middle of the ball game, it's not over yet.'

You may feel that you have become exceedingly vulnerable and you have taken a stand and at the moment people are laughing at you and scoffing at you and you feel that there is nothing to live for. Will God ever come to your rescue and vindicate you?

These men in Daniel became vulnerable, they just said, 'Test your servants for ten days' (1:12). The princes over them sincerely couldn't understand their request. Don't expect the world to understand you either. But that is not the end of the story. They were vindicated men, we read in verse 18, 'At the end of the time set by the king to bring them in, the chief official presented them to Nebuchadnezzar.' We find them first of all vindicated with reference to the authorities. Verse 19 says, 'The king talked with them, and he found none equal to Daniel, Hananiah, Mishael and Azariah.' They were vindicated with reference to their appearance. How do we know that? Well, back in verse 10 the official had said, 'I am afraid of my lord the king, who has assigned your food and drink. Why should he see you looking worse than the other young men of your age?' but now they found none equal to them. They were vindicated with reference to their apprehension. 'In every matter of wisdom and understanding about which the king questioned them, he found them ten times better than all the magicians and enchanters in his whole kingdom' (1:10). In other words, they were vindicated with reference to their autonomy—that is they were being independent and having self-control and being true to themselves. They were trusting a sovereign God who put them where they were and gave them the gifts that they had and gave them the convictions they had. It paid off. They were vindicated.

You must know the little chorus:

> Dare to be a Daniel,
> Dare to stand alone,
> Dare to have a purpose firm,
> Dare to make it known.

We would never have heard of these four men had they not been true to themselves, had they not the courage to be themselves, had they not been governed by conviction.

You have a gift nobody else has. There is a place nobody can fill but you and God has put you where you are for a purpose; he has made you like you are for a purpose. Don't blow it—to thine own self be true.

Chapter 14

'But if not' Faith

DANIEL 3

Shadrach, Meshach and Abednego were being trained for authentic leadership, although they may not have known it at the time. There are two kinds of leadership—authentic leadership and passive leadership. Authentic leadership is that which is exceedingly rare today for most leaders are passive leaders. Most leaders are followers. A typical leader of today's generation is one who wets his finger, holds it up into the air, sees which way the wind is blowing and then runs out in front and says he is leading where people are going anyway, only to get the credit. But what is needed is authentic leadership, and this is determined by how we react to temptation and testing. Shadrach, Meshach and Abednego were to undergo now a real trial greater than the one that we looked at in the last chapter.

Here were three men that decided to stand up and be counted. How they would react to this trial would determine whether they could be trusted with a higher level of spirituality and what can only be called authentic leadership. Jesus said, 'Whoever can be trusted with very little can also be trusted with much' (Lk 16:10). The difference between temptation and trial is simply this—testing is when God wants to bring the best out of you; temptation is when Satan wants to bring the worst out of you. These three men were to undergo severe testing and trial. Now if you try to be a leader on your own, you will probably fail because the kind of leadership to which we are called is not something that we are born to. Spiritual leadership is a grace not a gift. It is inner strength, not a position. Not something you do as a job, but something you are. In the last chapter, we saw that they purposed in their hearts not to defile themselves with the royal table and wine, and passing that examination enabled them now to be trusted with a deeper kind of trial. How are we changed from glory to glory? I wish I could say to you today that it could happen simply because you decide you are going to pray more or because you go forward in a service and ask somebody to pray for you. I don't underestimate how much God can use those things but I can tell you candidly I have not discovered a way to be changed from glory to glory apart from severe testing.

What Shadrach, Meshach and Abednego faced now was a trial that would be more severe than anything they had ever experienced. We all want faith like these men. We want the faith of Abraham but we don't like Abraham's suffering. But if we are going to go to the university of the Holy Spirit it means that we must first come up through school first, and that is through testing.

A few years ago, shortly after we first came to Westminster, I began preaching from the book of James. 'Consider it pure joy, my brothers, whenever you face trials of many kinds' (Jas 1:2). I was able to see from looking at that verse in considerable detail how it is that even at the natural level we don't go to university till we have had A levels, we don't have A levels until we have GCSE's (then it was O levels), and passing one examination at a time is what qualifies us for a higher kind. This is true spiritually, and right in the middle of preaching in that particular section my wife and I were to undergo what at the time seemed to be a very major trial. We had not been perfect examples of 'dignifying the trial', a phrase I coined during that time. Instead of murmuring and complaining God wants us to count it all joy when we fall into trials, and I have to tell you that we had not

done that. In the realisation that we were homesick to go
back to America, though God had put us in Westminster,
we were not examples of what God wanted us to be.

One evening I discovered that we couldn't use our
American driving licences. I had been using mine for
the time we were at Oxford before coming into London.
I thought it would still be valid but I found out this was
not so when I got caught speeding. Scotland Yard called
me and told me not to drive my car.

I said to Louise, 'I've got something to tell you, it's not
going to be very pleasant. You know I'm preaching on
dignifying the trial and God has given us a dandy.'

She said, 'Before you tell me, I have to tell you that
our washing machine just broke down, the drier just
broke down and we can't get it repaired for three weeks.
I want to go back to America.'

I said, 'Sit down, we're not going anywhere right now.
We can't even drive the car.'

She said, 'What do you mean? We have to go and get
our child.' I told her about our driving licences.

I said, 'Look, we have been murmurers and com-
plainers ever since we have been in London, and we
have got to dignify this trial. We may never have
another like it, and here is an opportunity to grow in
grace and I'd like you to pray with me now that we will
dignify this trial.'

Up to then every kind of trial we ever had I just
wanted to battle through. I was like the predestinarian
who fell down the stairs—he mopped his brow and said,
'I'm glad that's over.' I never got anywhere through a
trial but this time I said, 'Let's dignify it.' Those days
were hard I have to tell you. I had to take fresh driving
lessons. I have a friend who has a pilot's licence in
America. He said it was easier to get a pilot's licence in
America than a British driving licence. I had to go to
driving school and even had a woman instructor! (You
will appreciate that ordeal if you come from my kind of
church background.) We would not love to go through
those days again but, hard though they were, I discovered

a higher level of joy than I had ever known. A peace, an insight into Scripture, and it wasn't long until we had a real trial on our hands. We go from A to B and B to C in being changed from glory to glory.

Shadrach, Meshach and Abednego had passed their first test and now King Nebuchadnezzar wanted one religion. It can only be called pressurised conformity. False religion wants you to conform, that is, do it because everybody does it, and there is a possibility of a trend in Britain at this moment whereby the blasphemy law could be changed so it would be illegal to witness to Jews and to Muslims because it's all one way to God no matter which way you do it. This is what King Nebuchadnezzar wanted. Paul says, 'Do not conform any longer to the pattern of this world, but be transformed by the renewing of your mind' (Rom 12:2). Phillips' translation puts it, 'Don't let the world squeeze you into its mould.' God is in the process of making each of us more like Jesus. How does he do that? It is through his testing us, his refining us, through suffering and trial.

What we have here with Shadrach, Meshach and Abednego was a pressurised conformity being matched by a fearless courage. The obedience of the world is always through peer pressure. Motivation by fear. They want you to be afraid like they are and what the world wants is not only conformity but uncritical conformity, so that here, as soon as they would hear the sound of the horn, flute, zither, lyres, harp, pipes and all kinds of music they must fall down. They not only want uncritical conformity but instant conformity. The world doesn't really want you to think for yourself. Somebody has said that 5% of the world really think, another 5% think that they think, the other 90% don't think even if you kill them! Someone has said 5% make things happen, another 5% watch things happen, the other 90% never know what's going on. The word in Daniel was, as soon as they heard the sound of the music, all the peoples fell down.

But these three men marched to the beat of a different

drum. There now emerges another element of the story. I can only call it jealousy. We read in verse 8, 'At this time some astrologers came forward and denounced the Jews.' They weren't happy about the fact that Shadrach, Meshach and Abednego had been vindicated and exalted. They were jealous of them and were waiting for an opportunity to get at them. When you are exalted and something good happens to you, you discover enemies you never knew you had. Paul said, 'Rejoice with those who rejoice, mourn with those who mourn,' but it is easier to find those who will weep with you than those who will rejoice with you. Some people are jealous of your face: some people are jealous of your race, some are jealous of your lace, some are jealous of your place, but those who conformed and fell down and worshipped were jealous of their grace. Nebuchadnezzar would never have known about Shadrach, Meshach and Abednego, but they were reported. You take your stand and Satan will always find somebody to report you, or to make you look bad. They said to the king in verse 12, 'There are some Jews whom you have set over the affairs of the province of Babylon—Shadrach, Meshach and Abednego—who pay no attention to you, O king. They neither serve your gods nor worship the image of gold you have set up.'

Abraham Lincoln once said, 'If the end brings me out all right, what is set against me won't amount to anything. If the end brings me out wrong, ten angels swearing I was right would make no difference.' Shadrach, Meshach and Abednego became the objects of a pursued contempt—someone was out to get them. A leader in the making must experience this sooner or later, being the object of contempt. How you handle that will determine whether you are a real leader.

Peter said, 'Do not be surprised at the painful trial you are suffering, as though something strange were happening to you. But rejoice that you participate in the sufferings of Christ, so that you may be overjoyed when his glory is revealed' (1 Pet 4:12–13). And so it is a time like this if you are insulted, the Spirit of glory and of God rests upon you. You may not think it, you may not feel anything, but those are the times when you are being prepared for a grace whereby God can trust you with a level of power that perhaps you have wanted but there are no shortcuts to it.

So Shadrach, Meshach and Abednego, when they heard the sound of the music, stayed put. Everybody else fell down, they stayed standing. An enraged Nebuchadnezzar offered them another chance but he could see by the looks on their faces that they weren't going to accept it, so he just said, 'What god will be able to rescue you from my hand?' It is at this point we find that they answer his question. They put it like this, 'Oh Nebuchadnezzar, we do not need to defend ourselves,' and as the Authorised Version puts it 'Our God whom we serve is able to deliver us ... But if not ... we will not serve thy gods.'

Back in the hills of Kentucky I can remember a sweet lady, who had been going through a real trial, standing up in a prayer meeting. She put this question to the group, 'Do you have the "but if not" faith'? Our God is able to deliver us, *but if not* we will not bow down. So their answer was characterised by a personal conviction with regard to the nature of God.

If you asked Shadrach, Meshach and Abednego, they would say two things about God. One is that he is able, our God is able to deliver us. The second thing is that God is free. They took pressure off God so that God was free to do what he wanted to do. You haven't come truly to know God until you have, so to speak, set him free. When you set God free from having to answer your prayer, you are free. For the greatest freedom is having nothing to prove. Are you one of those Christians who is always having to prove something—you're striving, you're trying to perform? Are you having to prove something? Shadrach, Meshach and Abednego had set God free. You need to come to the place where you see that God has a will of his own. He is sovereign. He may answer your prayer, he may not. He may fulfil your ambition, he may not. Maybe you are one of those who says that if God does this for you then you'll do such and such for him, but that's bargaining with God and trying to manipulate him. You set him free and you are free.

Make up your mind

So we see that these three men were characterised by a prior commitment, they decided long before what they would do. Courage like this is planned in advance. By a prior commitment Jesus said, 'Watch and pray so that you will not fall into temptation' (Mt 26:41). A lot of people say they pray about things and then watch, and then if temptation comes they want to blame God for it. Jesus said, 'watch and pray so that you will not fall into temptation.' The apostle Paul said, 'Make no provision for the flesh, to fulfil the lust thereof.' Billy Sunday used to say the reason Christians fall into sin is because they treat temptation like strawberries and cream instead of a rattle snake. Real strength is not in seeing how close you can get to temptation without yielding, it is avoiding the temptation altogether. When there is that kind of commitment, and temptation comes, you don't have to pray about it. Do you think that when Nebuchadnezzar put the proposition to them, they looked at each other and said, 'Well, we had better talk about this'? Do you think Meshach spoke up and said, 'Just a minute, King, I want to talk to these two. I've been having problems with them lately'? They didn't need to look at each other and wink or nudge, no, they looked straight at the King and said, 'We don't have to answer you, we don't have to defend ourselves, we can tell you right now.'

There are some things you don't pray about, you just do them. You don't wait for God to give you the nudge when he has already spoken. In the words of the great hymn: 'What more can he say than to you he hath said?' They didn't need to think about it, they didn't need to pray about it. They lived by what I can only call the impulse of the Spirit. Their peers listened for music and they fell down. Shadrach, Meshach and Abednego listened to the impulse of the Spirit and they stood up. Unimpressed, the King had them bound and thrown into the burning fiery furnace.

When you're in the fire

I don't know if you can picture what it would be like. Have you ever looked inside a furnace or a boiler and seen the blazing red flames? The King was so angry he ordered those under him to heat it seven times hotter than usual. You know the devil always overreaches himself. We are told in verse 22, the King's command was so urgent and the furnace so hot that the flames killed the men who took them to the furnace. Maybe you are in the fire at the moment and those outside looking in cannot imagine how you can cope, or perhaps you are avoiding the fire because you say, 'I couldn't do it.' What we do know is that the King had these three men bound and thrown into the fire. But when we look at verse 24 I can only call it pleasant company. Chuck Colson once said that God doesn't promise to take us out of the fire but he gets into the fire with us. People ask me the question, 'Do you think that was really Jesus?' Well, I do. The Jesus I know just loves to do things like that, show up at a time when you think you can't go another day.

Once on a strong sea when the waves came on the Sea of Galilee the disciples looked and one said, 'Look who's here' and there was Jesus walking on the sea. After a night of fishing they heard a man shout from the shore, 'Have you caught any fish?' and it wasn't long before Peter looked and said, 'Look who's here.' And I reckon that Shadrach was rather enjoying himself being free of the rope and suddenly the other two shout at him, 'Shadrach, look who's here.' An enraged frustrated king, having just lost some of his men to the flames, now takes a peek into the fiery furnace. Shadrach, Meshach and Abednego saw the King looking in and they shouted at him, 'Look who's here.'

The question is, what will people see when you are in the fire? Will they be able to say to you, 'Well, look who's here!'? Will they see Jesus? Do you know this poem?

Twas not the truth you taught
  To you so clear, to me so dim,
But when you came to me you brought a sense of him.
  Yes from your eyes he beckoned me,
From your heart his love was shed,
  When I lost sight of you and saw the Christ instead.

And King Nebuchadnezzar ordered them to come out of the fire and then issued a decree that the people of any nation or language who said anything against the God of Shadrach, Meshach and Abednego be cut into pieces and their houses be turned into piles of rubble, for no other God could save in this way.

Whenever you are in the fire you know where to find Jesus. He is in the fire and if you want to be changed from glory to glory you may want the short cut and I wouldn't blame you for that. Just remember this, though: if you are ever given a trial, what can only be called a fiery trial, see it as God issuing to you an invitation on a silver platter to be changed from glory to glory. In the fire you will find Jesus there, you will find him to be real and you will be amazed and you'll say, 'Look who's here.' The 'but if not' faith overcomes impossible odds.

If you are typical of the 1980s, the odds are at some stage, you will be unfaithful in marriage. If you are typical of the 1980s at some stage you will be unscrupulous in business. The odds are you will not break out of your loneliness. The odds are you will not get over that grudge. But there is a faith that overcomes impossible odds. Our God is able to deliver us, but if not, we will not bow down.

But if not ...

What about those who aren't delivered? It is one thing to see the joy of how these men were set free. When I was a little boy my father would tell me the story and he would say, 'What was it that burned?' and I would say 'The rope.' The rope that had them bound was the only thing that burned. They were set free and it may be you are bound by something, you are tied by indifference, by intolerance, by bitterness, by a grudge, by sexual lust, and you are in bondage and you are asking God to set you free. You are in the fire, the rope will burn. But what about those in history who went into the flames but didn't come out? You know Hebrews chapter 11 describes the three Hebrew children in verse 34, they 'quenched the fury of the flames.' But that is not the only thing that depicts real faith because later on the same writer of Hebrews says, 'Others were tortured and refused to be released. Some faced jeers and flogging, while still others were chained and put in prison. They were stoned; they were sawn in two, they were put to death by the sword' (Heb 11:35–37). There is always the hope that when we are in the fire, somehow there will be the miracle. Sometimes we go right through it.

In 1555 in Balliol Ditch in Oxford, Bishop Hugh Latimer was tied back to back with young Bishop Nicholas Ridley, and the younger Bishop in his forties was scared and was trembling. They were hoping somehow it wouldn't happen but the flames were lit and they began to circle around the bodies. The seventy-year-old Latimer shouted back to Ridley, 'Fear not Master Ridley, and play the man, we shall this day light such a candle in England as such I trust shall never be put out.' The impact of those martyrdoms ensured that the faith stayed on British soil for another century. And so it may be that you are put through the fire and don't see the miracle that you would like to see.

In our congregation at Westminster Chapel there is a Chinese couple. Their little baby was born with a hole in the heart. They were waiting for open heart surgery and in the meantime we prayed for their little boy. We laid hands on him, we anointed him with oil and prayed and

prayed. Then came the day of the open heart surgery.
He was on the operating table for six hours and then the
surgeon was awakened in the middle of the night and
came back and opened him up again, and he died. It
would have been a miracle for little William Chang to
have been healed, but I say it was a greater miracle to see
the smile on the parents' faces when they said, 'We don't
question God.' In the words of Job, 'Though he slay me,
yet will I hope in him' (Job 13:15). Don't talk to me about a
health and wealth gospel, tell me if in the fire you can say,
'He is here, his presence is here.' God is able to deliver me
and if he doesn't I will not bow down, and if you are
trying to bargain with God and you say, 'I'll serve him if
he does this for me,' then turn in your badge. What is
needed in our day is the 'but if not' faith. Set him free;
he may deliver you, he may not. But serve him anyway.

There is on this globe at the moment suffering, going
into the fiery furnace, such as you and I in Britain are not
seeing. Sometime ago Richard Wurmbrand addressed a
church in Florida. It was a very upmarket church, formal,
very liturgical with a beautiful choir. Wurmbrand, from
Rumania, who had been in prison there, commented on
the beauty of the church, the service and the singing, but
he said, 'This morning I wonder if I could repeat to you
now the symphony that is being heard at the moment in
Rumania. I'm not sure I can repeat the symphony exactly
as it sounds, but you will have an idea as to what you can
hear at this moment in prisons in Rumania—Aaagh!'

There are those who are in the fire while we in our
comfort and ease ask for more of God and have not a
clue as to the kind of suffering some are going through.
The proof of vindication is not in what manner you are
delivered, but who people see with you when you are in
the fire. These men were being trained for leadership.
They passed their test. Will people be able to see you in
the fire and also comment 'Look who's here'?

Chapter 15

The Party's Over

DANIEL 5

You have heard the expression 'handwriting on the wall'. We are going to look at the origin of that phrase and its meaning.

As a little boy my father would tell me stories from the Bible, but it wasn't until I was a teenager, that I realised that the story of the sinking of the Titanic was not one of them, because it was told to me alongside all the rest. My father had grown up hearing of the sinking of the Titanic as a youngster and it made such an impact on him. We can see now how the theme of this section—Deckchairs on the Titanic—emerges in the book of Daniel. For early in this century there was to be a ship that would be unsinkable. The Titanic made its maiden voyage from this country to cross the Atlantic but hit an iceberg on the way, and the unthinkable happened.

Daniel chapter 5 is about two men and it is about the fall of the Babylonian kingdom. There is now a new king whose name is Belshazzar. Daniel is older in years and forgotten by the new king but at long last is called on again. The new king Belshazzar was the son of Nebuchadnezzar. As it would turn out Belshazzar would be the last Babylonian king. Now in chapter 2 and chapter 4 we learn that Daniel was given by the Holy Spirit an extraordinary ability to interpret dreams.

This is a gift that I think probably is not common

today, I have never understood my own dreams, I certainly don't understand my wife's dreams. Shortly after we were married she was saying every morning, 'You know I had the most brilliant thought in the middle of the night. I forgot it though.'

I said, 'Well you know they say you ought to write them down.' So she woke up one morning and said, 'I did it last night. I have written down a profound thought that I had in the middle of the night and I've got it here.' It read 'ELEPHANTITIS, FUN BUT NOT FUNNY.' We both laughed together. We needed Daniel!

Sometimes you have what you think are brilliant thoughts, then you look at them and you don't know what they mean. Nebuchadnezzar had a dream that he forgot entirely and he was going to kill his magicians if they couldn't think it up. They called for Daniel, he recalled the dream perfectly and also gave the interpretation. Daniel's interpretation of Nebuchadnezzar's dreams earned him the highest respect of the King. But now there is a new king. Belshazzar son of Nebuchadnezzar owed nothing to Daniel and showed no respect for his father's regard, nor for Daniel, nor the true God whom Nebuchadnezzar had come to affirm. Nebuchadnezzar became arrogant nonetheless and it was prophesied by Daniel that King Nebuchadnezzar would be humbled and be driven away from the people and eat grass like cattle. That is exactly what happened, but Nebuchadnezzar repented and then praised the Most High and affirmed the true God.

Though this had happened to Nebuchadnezzar, his son Belshazzar wanted nothing to do with it and Daniel was put to one side for a while. Belshazzar became an arrogant king but also a weak one. Something you ought to know about arrogant people—they are basically very weak. Belshazzar wanted to throw a party for the Babylonian elite to show how strong he was. And so we read 'King Belshazzar gave a great banquet for a

thousand of his nobles and drank wine with them'
(5:1). I think we could safely say it was a big room! So
the party began. He couldn't have done it at a worse
time.

Outside the walled city of Babylon the armies of
Darius, also known as Cyrus, were trying to capture the
city of Babylon. But the King had boasted, 'Our city of
Babylon is impenetrable.' Just as they had said of the
Titanic that it was unsinkable. When that Titanic
crashed into an iceberg, do you know what they did?
The captain of the ship ordered that the music continue
to play. He told everyone to eat, drink and be merry,
there is nothing to worry about, this is the Titanic, it is
unsinkable, God can't sink it. He ordered the bands to
keep on playing and that is essentially what King
Belshazzar did.

Here were the armies encircling the city but the
King said, 'Nothing to worry about,' and he throws a
party—to demonstrate his defiance and to prove his
confidence. I've said before the greatest freedom is
having nothing to prove, but Belshazzar had a lot to
prove and he wanted to put to rest the fears of his
supporters.

Now as we look at Daniel 5 there is one word that will
serve as a thread that holds the events together. It is the
word 'change'. And yet more than a change of government or administrations was at stake. There was to be
the downfall of the Babylonian king. We are talking
about the same Babylonians that had held Israel
hostage. They themselves were to be taken over by the
Medes and Persians. It would also be a happy change for
Daniel and eventually Israel. You can imagine from
Daniel's point of view that the years under Belshazzar
must have been a very difficult era for him. He had to
wait on God to act. You may feel that you have former
days that were outstanding but at the moment you are
put to one side and you are not being used as you once

were. The invitations aren't coming. There's no need for you, it would seem, and yet you have been refined, honed, and prepared by the Holy Spirit. You wonder, 'Will God ever use me again?' That was Daniel.

Another way to look at chapter 5 is put by Jesus in these words, 'Woe to the world because of the things that cause people to sin! Such things must come, but woe to the man through whom they come!' (Mt 18:7). We are dealing here with a great mystery, how God was grieved with Israel and judged Israel and the result was the Babylonian captivity. But now God decided to judge Babylon. This is a mystery which I don't claim to understand. God may chasten his church but he will also turn on those who scorn and deride his chastening of the church. So God allowed the King of Babylon to capture the gold and the silver goblets from Solomon's temple in Jerusalem. Those goblets were used only by the tribe of Levi and the priesthood, but when Belshazzar gave orders to bring them into his party for the godless to use and they toasted to the gods of gold, silver, bronze, iron, wood and stone, God didn't like it one bit. Enough is enough. This is a lesson for all of us at the present time to warn us and to encourage us to remember that God's judgement may well be on the church generally, but those who scoff at historic Christian faith, church leaders who scoff at our Christian heritage, politicians who scoff at the church and that which is sacred, journalists, TV comedians who scorn what is sacred, will one day face the folly of their ridicule when God decides to roll up his sleeves and let the world know what he thinks of that.

That night Belshazzar gave the party and it gives us a glimpse of how God will sooner or later intervene in life. In the life of a nation, in the life of a church, in the lives of individuals. So on that night when Belshazzar gave his party there is reason to believe it was a night of debauchery, because we read in verse 2, 'While Belshazzar was drinking his wine, he gave orders to bring in the gold and silver goblets that Nebuchadnezzar his father had taken from the temple in Jerusalem, so that the king and his nobles, his wives and his concubines might drink from them.' It was a night of frivolity, sensuality and immorality; monogamous marriage, fidelity and morality simply were not on the menu. It was a night of desecration, to treat that which is sacred or religious with scorn and derision, as when the world treats the Bible generally with contempt, or when church leaders forget our Christian heritage and treat biblical Christianity with contempt. It was a night of drunkenness because according to verse 2 it wasn't until Belshazzar was drinking wine that he felt brave enough to do what he did when he brought in the goblets from the temple. He couldn't have done it sober perhaps, but he needed a little drink to show that he was different from his father Nebuchadnezzar, he wasn't going to bow down to the God of Daniel. He wanted to show contempt for the God of the temple by drinking with the gold and silver goblets that had been taken.

It was a night of dreaming. We all dream, as Kipling put it, 'If you can dream and not make dreams your master.' This turned out to be a night of delusion. It was the worst time to throw a party. It was Belshazzar's way of escaping from reality and refusing to face the obvious; refusing to face the inevitable. Are you living in a dream world? Maybe you don't escape by drink, maybe you don't escape by drugs, maybe you don't escape by sex, but you live in a fantasy world. You live in a world in which you want to do your own thing, and that is your party, and you want it to go on for ever. But it was a night of discontinuity for that dream became a living nightmare when all of a sudden, 'The fingers of a human hand appeared and wrote on the plaster of the wall' (5:5).

The party's over

This can only be described as a sovereign intervention of
God. We're told it was a sudden intervention. Suddenly
the fingers of a human hand appeared. Sometimes God
works gradually and takes a long time (Gal 4:4). Sometimes God works suddenly: 'suddenly the Lord will
come to his temple' (Mal 3:1). We are told when the day
of Pentecost was fully come, suddenly there came a
sound from heaven like a rushing mighty wind, and we
are told of the second coming, that it will take place
suddenly. And Proverbs 29:1 says, 'A man who remains
stiff-necked after many rebukes will suddenly be
destroyed—without remedy.'

Sometimes God works suddenly and that is what
happened here. Yet it was a silent intervention. We just
read that there was the handwriting on the wall and yet
there was something almost unspectacular about it, no
noise, no fanfare, no introduction. Unusual though it
was, there was something lacklustre about it; it was just
there. But the style of handwriting on the wall stopped
everything. The frolicking, the noise, the laughter, the
sensuality, the music, the drinking, the blasphemy stopped. Before you could count to ten there came an eerie
silence over that banquet hall. You could hear a pin
drop on the velvet carpet. The sound of silence sent the
signal—the party's over. It was a solemn intervention.

For the first time in recorded history we have an
account of a man being so scared that his knees knocked
together. You talk about change, his face turned pale. I
ask, 'Why was that?' We know that the King had his
enchanters, his magicians, and it was to be an unusual
party. Surely they had the Paul Daniels of that age who
could do their tricks, so why didn't the King suddenly
say, 'Well, look what my magicians have done now!' On
the contrary, as soon as he saw the handwriting on the
wall his face turned pale, his knees knocked together. I
say if God could by his finger change the countenance of

a king, what will it be like on that day when what John saw on the Isle of Patmos is fulfilled for all men? John was given a sneak preview of the second coming of Jesus. He said, 'Look, he is coming with the clouds, and every eye will see him, even those who pierced him; and all the peoples of the earth will mourn because of him' (Rev 1:7). John said 'The kings of the earth, the princes, the generals, the rich, the mighty, and every slave and every free man hid in the cave and among the rocks of the mountains. They called to the mountains and the rocks, "Fall on us and hide us from the face of him who sits on the throne and from the wrath of the Lamb".' For the day of the wrath will come, and who shall be able to stand when God says to a whole world, 'the party is over'?

Paul said, 'If only for this life we have hope in Christ, we are to be pitied more than all men' (1 Cor 15:19). The Bible teaches there is a heaven and there is a hell and if there were no hell there would be no reason for Jesus to die on a cross. The Bible is summed up in John 3:16 which Martin Luther called 'the Bible in a nutshell'. It may be that you are sitting on the deckchairs of the Titanic and you are living in your own world as though it would go on for ever, when suddenly God will say, 'The party is over, right now you give an account'—no further warning. When my father used to tell me the story of the Titanic he would often break into tears as he told what happened just before the ship went under. Those who lived to tell the story say that the same band that had been ordered to strike up the music and encourage everybody, just before the end played 'Nearer My God to Thee'. There will come a day when you'll come to grips with what really matters. Where will you be 100 years from now?

So on that night it was a strategic intervention. How do we know that? Well as I said, at that precise moment King Cyrus Darius discovered a way that they could get into the city. It had been called the city that could never be conquered. The hanging gardens of the ancient city of Babylon are known as one of the seven wonders of the world. The wall of the city was so wide that two chariots could go side by side completely around it. They weren't the slightest bit worried about anybody getting into that city. However, there was one thing nobody had thought about. A river went right through the city. It went under a walled bridge and the army of Darius came up with an ingenious plan. They went upstream a good way and they dammed the river which made a lake and diverted the water so that the river went dry and King Darius's army walked on foot under the bridge and began to conquer the city from within.

So Cyrus's army were building that dam upstream while the Babylonian aristocracy came to grips with what God wanted. For God knows everything that is going on in this world and can use the wise and the unwise to accomplish his end. It is God that exalts nations, it is God that abases. The nations to him are but a drop in the bucket. Now the interesting thing is that God might have done all this and let it happen without even letting Belshazzar know just an hour or two in advance what was happening. So it was a secret intervention in that God had a message that he wanted to give to everybody just before the end and he wanted to do it his way. So here was the handwriting on the wall.

What do the words mean? Everybody knew what they meant. They knew the words were, 'Me-ne, me-ne, te-kel, u-par-sin.' The word me-ne simply meant numbered, it was in Aramaic, everybody knew the word. They didn't need a dictionary, they didn't need Daniel to translate it. Te-kel means weighed. U-par-sin means shared. So they knew what the words meant, and yet they didn't know because Belshazzar knew in his heart of hearts there had to be a hidden meaning. So he called out for the enchanters, astrologers and diviners to be brought and said to these wise men of Babylon, 'Whoever reads this writing and tells me what it means will be clothed in

purple and have a gold chain placed around his neck,
and he will be made the third highest ruler in the
kingdom' (5:7). Those enchanters wanted to figure out
the meaning. This was their chance for promotion. But,
they were baffled.

Daniel was needed again and yet they didn't send for
him at first. I suppose the last person Belshazzar wanted
to send for was Daniel. He wanted to defy his father's
God, the God of Israel. It may be that you are waiting to
be noticed and to be used and they are sending for
everybody else but you. Don't worry about those who
are sent for first. Jesus said, 'Many who are first will be
last, and many who are last will be first' (Mt 19:30), and
if you have kept humble and if you have submitted to
God's chastening, if you have refused to be bitter and
refused to exalt yourself but you have waited on God's
time, there will come a day when nobody but you will be
needed. Victor Hugo said, 'Like the trampling of a
mighty army, so is the force of an idea whose time has
come.' And I can paraphrase that, 'Like a trampling of a
mighty army so is the force of one's gift, so is the force of
one's calling, so is the force of one's personality whose
time has come.' Daniel had been refined over the years,
he had been put to one side, and wondered, 'Will God
ever need me again?' Daniel was waiting for this
moment, and though there is no doubt he had been
refined by the Holy Spirit as God chiselled away that
which was unlike Jesus would be, Daniel was still in
preparation.

We all still need preparation. You never outgrow the
need of preparation, but you may ask the question,
'How will they know about me if I don't pull some
strings?' Well they came looking for Daniel and they'll
come looking for you. Who do you suppose gave the
word about Daniel? It says the Queen, but we know
from the Hebrew it was really the Queen mother. Do
you see the implications? The Queen mother told
Belshazzar to send for Daniel because she was the wife of

Nebuchadnezzar. She knew about Daniel and we learn later that so did Belshazzar. It makes me think of that story in 2 Kings 5 when there was the little servant girl who wanted to see her master Naaman healed of leprosy and she said, 'Go and see Elisha.' How will they know about you? It may be that you'll be sent for by the Queen mother or by a chalet maid, but they'll find you. God has a way of bringing right to the top those who are ready for it. The worst thing that can happen is to succeed before you are ready, and only God knows when you are ready.

Well, here comes Daniel but this King Belshazzar, silly man, promises him a gold chain. Can you see Daniel wanting to wear a big gold chain? Can you see this man Daniel actually being tempted by things like that?

What is so sad is that there are those in the ministry today and in the clergy, speaking generally, who are motivated by material gain. And you wonder why there is a dearth of greatness and why there is an absence of unction—it is because small men scrambling for power can be motivated by the sort of thing that Belshazzar thought would motivate Daniel. Daniel said, 'Keep your gifts for someone else, but I'll read the writing.'

I have been thinking recently that, with all the scandals in America with the TV evangelists, you know the one man who has been untouched by it all is Billy Graham. He has come out proving that a man can be humble and God will use him. When we were on holiday in Fort Lauderdale I met Billy Graham's daughter, Gigi Tchividjian, and we went out with her and her husband for ice cream one evening. I turned to her and said, 'Gigi, what is your father's secret?' She said, 'It's very simple. When he was a little boy in Sunday school they sang this chorus: Let me do each day's work for Jesus with eternity's values in view.'

And I think of small men today who are just wanting instant recognition, fame and fortune. The apostle Paul says, 'Knowing the terror of the Lord we persuade men'

(2 Cor 5:11). What is needed is a generation of Christians who are not motivated by small things. Here was Daniel's secret, he said, 'Keep your gifts.' And what Daniel now says to Belshazzar is in my opinion a sneak preview of that final judgement: 'Man is destined to die once, and after that to face judgment' (Heb 9:27).

First of all Daniel's speech was a rehearsal of what Belshazzar already knew. He says in verse 18, 'O king, the Most High God gave your father Nebuchadnezzar sovereignty and greatness and glory and splendour.' Daniel brings to the mind of Belshazzar what Belshazzar already knew, the sovereignty of God.

What do you know about the sovereignty of God? Are you aware that God has a will of his own? God isn't manipulated by us, we don't tell God what to do. When you come to terms with the God of the Bible you will bow before him and recognise that he is the same God who once said to Moses, 'I will have mercy on whom I will have mercy, and I will have compassion on whom I will have compassion' (Ex 33:19). This view of the sovereignty of God has almost perished from the earth. Daniel said, 'This is something you need to know, Belshazzar,' it is not only a rehearsal but a reminder because, as he says in verse 22, 'But you his son, O Belshazzar, have not humbled yourself, though you knew all this.' It now comes out that Belshazzar knew what he was doing.

So now there came the meanings, three things according to Daniel. First, God determines the number of our days. (And that is true of all of us, by the way.) Second, Belshazzar, God has assessed your term. You have been found wanting. Third, the party is over. Your time is up, your kingdom is divided and given to the Medes and the Persians. 'This very night your life will be demanded from you' (Lk 12:20).

But something that interests me is that despite what Daniel said to Belshazzar, Belshazzar still clothed Daniel in purple and a gold chain was put around his neck.

Belshazzar was true to his word, and yet I just wonder if in rewarding Daniel, somehow Belshazzar was making a last minute plea, begging. We know that will happen on the day of judgement. Jesus said, 'Many will say to me on that day, "Lord, Lord, did we not prophesy in your name, and in your name drive out demons and perform many miracles?" Then I will tell them plainly, "I never knew you. Away from me, you evil doers!' (Mt 7:22–23). So that very night Belshazzar was slain and Darius the Mede took over the kingdom. A new regime, a new king came in overnight. God can bring about change gradually or suddenly. A city that could not be penetrated was penetrated and the unsinkable Titanic went to the bottom of the sea.

Are you having a party? Is life for you one big party? I don't mean by that that you are living in luxury and ease, but are you doing your own thing, are you withdrawn into your little world and thinking it is going to go on for ever? Don't be a fool. At any moment Jesus himself will say, 'This very night your life will be demanded from you.'

Chapter 16

An Open Secret

DANIEL 6

This is the best known story from the book of Daniel—
Daniel in the lions' den. As a result of those who were
threatened by Daniel's success, and now with the plan of
the new King Darius to exalt him and make him to be
head over the whole kingdom, there were jealous men
who said that it could not be. The only way they could
do anything to overrule this decision was to find something against Daniel with reference to the law of his
God. So they conned the King into making a decree
according to the laws of the Medes and Persians which
cannot be annulled, that anybody who praised any God
other than King Darius would be put in the lions' den.

This did not threaten Daniel. He got down on his
knees and prayed, giving thanks to God as he had done
before. Then the King realised the trap set for Daniel
but nevertheless had to abide by the law. Daniel is
thrown into the lions' den only to be miraculously
delivered. According to Daniel, God sent his angel and
shut the mouths of the lions.

The source of opposition

I want us to take up a point that I referred to earlier
(Chapter 14), that is: Satan always overreaches himself.
Daniel knew who the real enemy was, and it is a sign of

great spiritual progress when we recognise who the real enemy is; that way we do not take opposition personally. Paul recognised the real enemy when he said, 'Our struggle is not against flesh and blood' (Eph 6:12). Now as long as we are struggling against flesh and blood then we are going to take opposition personally. But Paul says, 'Our struggle is not against flesh and blood, but against the rulers ... against the powers of this dark world'—in a word the enemy is the devil, and whenever you realise that he is the source of your opposition it will change your whole outlook, and will make you see that those who are opposing you are simply tools of the devil, and if you react to them personally the devil has won. But if you will take the cue from the Holy Spirit to go on and pray like you have never prayed before, and give thanks to God and show courage such as you never thought you had within you, you will find that the devil will overreach himself. He was the architect of the crucifixion of Jesus. Satan entered Judas Iscariot and then came the time when Jesus was actually hanging on the cross and Satan thought he had won, only to discover at the end of the day that that was God's way of promoting the glory of God. We are told in 1 Corinthians 2:8, 'None of the rulers of this age understood it, for if they had, they would not have crucified the Lord of glory,' but Satan overreached himself in the crucifixion of Jesus and that was the pattern you see right through history. We have seen how with Shadrach, Meshach and Abednego, all that Satan did there backfired, even those who made the furnace seven times hotter were burned. We learn now in the case of Daniel coming out of the lions' den that those who falsely accused Daniel were then thrown in and before they reached the floor of the den the lions over-powered them and crushed all their bones. As a result of everything Daniel was to be exalted more than ever.

We need to realise that it is the devil who is against us, not that person, not that intimidating boss at work, not that difficult one you have to live with, not that situation that you are dreading. Satan wants to get at you but if you will go on as before and pray and give thanks and show courage, God will do that which you never dreamed possible. He will shut the mouths of the lions and Satan will be seen to overreach himself. It always happens.

Normally anybody let down into the lions' den would be dealt with in about thirty seconds, and we see that from verse 24. You may be interested to know that in the ancient near east the sport of kings was lion hunting, the pit in which lions were kept provided a trouble free method of disposing of undesirable members of society. The lions' den had two entrances, a ramp down which the animals would enter or a hole in the roof by which they were normally fed. I'm not sure whether Daniel was thrown in from the top or the side, but there was only one way out, unless someone let down a rope. It was to prevent such a rescue that a stone was brought and sealed by the King as we see in verse 17, 'the king sealed it with his own signet ring and with the rings of the nobles, so that Daniel's situation might not be changed.'

What God did for Daniel he will do for you, so that the trial you dread and the situation in a few days' time you need not fear. Jesus said, 'I am with you always, to the very end of the age' (Mt 28:20), and 'Never will I leave you; never will I forsake you' (Heb 13:5).

Daniel's secret

I want us to deal with the question, what do you suppose was Daniel's secret? It has to be said that Daniel, Shadrach, Meshach and Abednego were exceedingly rare men. It is not every day that you meet someone who conveys the presence of greatness. I don't know about you, but I have a peculiarity in that whenever I am in the presence of one I deem to be truly great I instinctively ask, 'What is their secret?' I want to absorb anything I can. If I find out it is just because they have a high IQ or they had educational advantages, that is no encouragement to me. But if I can find out that there is something about them which could be shared, then I want to take full advantage of it. Whenever I get the chance to meet somebody great I want to learn his secret.

I had a privilege that I doubt that any minister of this century has had. In the providence of God, soon after we came to Westminster Chapel, Dr Martyn Lloyd-Jones was still around and he made me welcome to come into his home and I took full advantage of it. For some four years I was in and out of his house, and every Thursday for two hours, I would go over what I intended to preach the following Sunday. Friday night, Sunday morning, Sunday night, I doubt any minister in the history of the Christian church had a greater opportunity than I to sit at the feet of a man like that. What an honour it was for me to be spoon-fed by him. I will never be able to tie his shoes when it comes to preaching. Perhaps the greatest thing he taught me was to be mastered by the text, so that one never imports anything to the text. An expository preacher must let the text call for what needs to be preached and that way one is consistent and true to Scripture.

So what was Daniel's secret? Earlier we saw the overthrow of Babylon and a new king. Now Darius the Mede was none other than Cyrus the Persian, the man who would one day allow Israel to return. Despite the change of government, Daniel continued to enjoy royal favour. When we get to heaven we can find out just why the new king was attracted to Daniel. It may be that the new king heard about Daniel's prophecy of Belshazzar. Whatever, we know that Daniel was not a threat to the new King and there was a real friendship. Real friendship is when there is no threat to each other. When you see one another as a threat then there will always be tension. But the problem was, not all felt that way about Daniel. He had exceptional grace and he so distinguished himself by his qualities that the king planned to set him over the whole kingdom, and that was too much for his peers.

We might wish that this were a world where able people were always appreciated. We might wish this were a world whereby elderly people were always appreciated. Did you realise Daniel now is probably seventy years old? We might wish that the church were a place where godly people were always appreciated. It may be that you have taken a stand and you feel that if you take a stand for God, somehow everybody is going to admire you and clap their hands. But it could rather be that when you take a stand for Jesus Christ you may have imputed to a lot of people around you a level of spirituality that they just don't have.

Here, Daniel was being exalted but we are told that there were those who couldn't cope with that. Daniel was one of three administrators over 120 satraps (a satrap is probably the ancient equivalent of a member of the House of Lords, like a regional prince). A lot of people wanted Daniel's job and did their best to get him fired.

Well now, how were Daniel's jealous peers going to get at Daniel? They had three things going for them. The first, the king's ego. You see all people are by nature very proud, and even though the king admired Daniel, he had his weakness and so they played on the king's ego. Have you noticed how when people want to turn others against you, they play into the big ego and that's a hard one to reckon with. So they said to the king, 'O King Darius live for ever! The royal administrators, prefects, satraps, advisors and governors have all agreed that the king should issue an edict and enforce the decree that anyone who prays to any god or man during the next thirty days, except to you, O king, shall be thrown into the lions' den' (vv 6, 7). He was trapped. The second thing going for these men was an inflexible tradition. It was known as the law of the Medes and Persians. It's an expression that comes out of the book of Esther, and the law of the Medes and Persians could not be annulled once it was signed. It was the same as an oath. It could not be taken back. Perhaps you have discovered that the law of the Medes and the Persians is not something that is only in 600BC; perhaps you have found the law of the Medes and Persians in your church. Do you know the last seven words of a dying church?— 'We never did it this way before.'

Soon after we came to Westminster Chapel, twelve years ago, we were coming up to the Good Friday service and it was going to be my first one. About three days before I got a telephone call from one of the deacons who had been at Westminster Chapel for 218 years!

He said, 'Dr Kendall, you are going to be conducting the Good Friday service aren't you?'

I said, 'Yup.'

He said, 'Just one or two comments about our Good Friday service.'

'Sure,' I said.

He said, 'Now, Dr Lloyd-Jones always referred to his Good Friday sermon as a meditation.'

'Well, thank you,' I said. 'Thank you very much, I appreciate your phone call. God bless you brother.'

'Oh, one other thing,' he said. 'When Dr Lloyd-Jones preached on Good Friday he didn't preach quite as long as he did on Sunday.'

'I see, well that's very useful to know, thank you very much. God bless you, thank you for your phone call.'

'One other thing, on Good Friday Dr Lloyd-Jones always chose as the second hymn, "O Sacred Head Sore Wounded."'

I said, 'Is there anything more?'

You know that dear man is one of my best friends today. He is a sweet man, I love him. It is just to show that there are those who are traditional and naturally like things to go on as they always did, and so remember when there are those who want to keep a tradition up that they can be very good people.

The third thing though that these jealous peers had going for them to get Daniel out was Daniel's own first love. They knew about his love for God. 'We will never find any basis for charges against this man Daniel unless it has something to do with the law of his God' (6:5).

Do you know what it is like to have those against you who need to justify it by turning things into a theological issue? Perhaps they know that is the only way they can recruit support against you. They may play into the fears—or pride—of innocent people, like Darius, to get at you. Daniel chapter 6 will be precious to you.

As soon as the king had signed the document Daniel knew that he had been framed. King Darius did not realise that an ulterior motive prompted this show of loyalty. He had no idea at the time they were after Daniel. Now as for Daniel himself he had a decision on his hands. It was not a question of a positive sin which he should not commit but a positive duty which he should not omit, as Joyce Baldwin put it in her commentary on Daniel (Tyndale Commentary, IVP).

Perhaps someone has come to you and said, 'All I'm asking you to do is such and such for about a month, that's all. What's a month?' What was Daniel's decision? Verse 10 says 'When Daniel learned that the decree had been published, he went home to his upstairs room where the windows opened toward Jerusalem. Three times a day he got down on his knees and prayed, giving thanks to his God, just as he had done before.'

Why did he make this decision? I think there were two reasons. The first was, why should he betray God who had been so faithful to him? And secondly, Daniel knew that even if he did everything right for thirty days this would not end their vendetta against him. Once a person turns against you there is not a lot you can do about it. I think that is one of the things that I've had to learn the hard way—if I have made any mistake over the years it was trying to please those who were against me. Doing my very best, bending over backwards and doing everything. Daniel knew, no matter what he did, they were out to get him. Once a person is dead against you,

you have got to come to the place where you live by the principle of John 5:44—it's God's praise that counts.

It is at this point that we discover Daniel's secret. It had something to do with God and the most encouraging thing of all is that it was not his ability at the natural level, which no doubt he also had. It was three things. First, his prayer life. Secondly, that his heart was free of bitterness. Third, his courage. And so it was an ordinary secret. Prayer takes discipline and Daniel had a regular time. It was an ordinary secret. Extraordinary man but an ordinary secret, it is something anybody can do. You see Daniel simply loved God so much that he gave time to him. We tell how much we care about another by how much time we give him. The secret of Daniel was not his intellect, it wasn't his personality, his visions, or even his ability to debate—it was his prayer life. There was nothing complex about Daniel. When he learned that the decree had been published he went home to his upstairs room where the windows opened toward Jerusalem. It was an open secret. He shared it with anybody. 'You want to know the secret?' Daniel says, 'Here it is, I'll give it to you.'

Louise and I had an old friend years ago when we first moved to Florida, her name was Mae—she is now in heaven. She made the best green beans that I ever ate in my life. I said to her, 'Mae, would you show Louise how to make your green beans?' 'Sure, I'd be glad to do it.' I was looking forward to coming home at the end of the day and having Mae's green beans by Louise's hands. However, they weren't quite the same! It wasn't because of Louise's lack of ability, or not following the recipe, but we found out that Mae wouldn't share her total secret recipe! There are people like that, who don't trust nobody!

Daniel didn't care, it was an open secret. Windows wide open and regular as clock work. We need to learn the joy of a daily disciplined prayer life. The trouble with the old negro spiritual, 'Every time I feel the Spirit

moving in my heart I'll pray,' is that most of us don't feel
moved that much to pray. If I waited until I was moved
to pray, I might pray once a month, but I'm not sure I
would then. I find it hard work, it takes discipline. If you
were a member of Westminster Chapel I would say you
need to spend thirty minutes a day on your knees. I
won't push the position, you can sit if you like, or stand!
But don't expect God to make it easy for you, as if to say,
'Well, Lord if you really want me to do it, it will easily fall
in place.' It's amazing how we manage to get to work on
time. We do anything it takes to be there. But when it
comes to giving God his time, that's different.

I remember once I felt this impulse to start getting up
at 5 o'clock in the morning to pray. I said, 'Lord, if you
really want me to get up at 5 o'clock in the morning I
want you to wake me up, then I'll be convinced that you
really want me to do it.' I forgot I said it and went to bed
and to sleep. In the middle of the night I woke up, my
mind was clear and I looked around at the clock and it
was dead on 5 o'clock. I thought, 'Well thank you Lord,
praise God,' and I prayed for the next couple of hours,
it was wonderful. That night I went to bed and said,
'Lord, do it again,' and I slept through to 8 o'clock the
next morning. God says, 'I did it once.' And I find I have
to discipline myself.

So Daniel didn't care who knew. It wasn't that he was
bragging, it wasn't a violation of Matthew 6, he was just
doing what he had always done. The second thing we
are told is, he got on his knees and prayed, giving thanks
to God, just as he had done before. Surely with this new
edict in operation he is not going to get on his knees and
thank God for this? He must be scared to death. No, he
goes on and there is only one reason for this and I've
thought about it for a long time. What enables a person
to give thanks to God in a time of intense trial, especially
if there is opposition or persecution? There is only one
way you can do it, when your heart is free of bitterness.
Daniel kept thanking God, and often the reason we can't

thank God is because we are angry with him. We say to God 'Why?' 'Why did you do this to me?' 'Why did you let this happen?' and as long as you have got that bitterness towards God then you are not going to discover the thanksgiving that was in Daniel.

Third was Daniel's courage. He kept it up just as he had done before. And so it all came out; the king said to Daniel, 'I don't know what to say. I'm sorry, I've set my signature to this decree, the law of the Medes and Persians cannot be changed. I am sorry but I've got to throw you into the den of lions.' Daniel says, 'All right, praise God.' Daniel goes in and the king is tossing and turning all night long. The last thing he says to Daniel is a prayer, 'May your God, whom you serve continually, rescue you!' (6:16). Meanwhile Daniel is just sleeping like a baby. Next morning at dawn an anguished king says, 'Daniel are you still there?' Daniel said, 'O king, live for ever! My God sent his angel, and he shut the mouths of the lions' (6:21–22).

The angel of the Lord encamps around those who fear him. I believe this with all my heart. Wherever I go an angel is with me.

You may dread work on a Monday morning, or your marriage is one long trial. Jesus said, 'I am with you' (Mt 28:20). Maybe you are living with people or working with them and it's a nightmare. 'Never will I leave you; never will I forsake you' (Heb 13:5). Maybe you're under financial pressure. 'My God will supply all your needs according to his glorious riches in Christ Jesus' (Phil 4:19). Maybe you have the dilemma of indecision. 'Your strength will equal your days' (Deut 33:25). Maybe you are in an impossible situation. Think of the old hymn:

> When through the deep waters I call thee to go,
>   The rivers of woe shall not overflow,
> For I will be with thee, thy trials to bless
>   And sanctify to thee thy deepest distress.

You'll see all over again Satan overreaching himself, and God will enable you to go through it and come back stronger than ever.